Fifth Grade

Everyday Mathematics®

Resource Book
Blackline Masters

**The University of Chicago
School Mathematics Project**

EVERYDAY LEARNING™

Chicago, Illinois

This material is based upon work supported by the National Science Foundation under Grant No. ESI-9252984. Any opinions, findings, and conclusions or recommendations expressed in this material are those of the authors and do not necessarily reflect the views of the National Science Foundation.

1 2 3 4 5 6 7 8 9 BP 02 01 00 99 98

Contents

Unit 1

Number

Theory

Parent Letter

Introduction to *Fifth Grade Everyday Mathematics*®

Everyday Mathematics offers students a broad background in mathematics. Some approaches and topics in this program may differ from those you encountered as a student. However, they are based on research results, field-test experiences, and the mathematics that students will need in the twenty-first century. Following are some highlights of *Fifth Grade Everyday Mathematics:*

- A problem-solving approach that uses mathematics in everyday situations
- Partner and small-group activities that promote cooperative learning
- Concepts and skills introduced and reviewed throughout the school year, promoting retention through a variety of exposures
- Development of concepts and skills through hands-on activities
- Opportunities for discussion and communicating mathematically
- Frequent practice using games to provide an alternative to tedious drills
- Opportunities for home and school partnerships

Fifth Grade Everyday Mathematics emphasizes the following content:

Algebra and Uses of Variables Creating number models; working with scientific calculators; squaring and unsquaring numbers; exploring variables in formulas.

Exploring Data and Chance Collecting, organizing, and analyzing data using bar graphs, line graphs, circle graphs, and stem-and-leaf plots.

Geometry and Spatial Sense Investigating angles and rotations; calculating area and volume; drawing to scale; introducing relationships of 2- and 3-dimensional figures; exploring new transformations that affect attributes of geometric shapes.

Measures and Measurement Using linear, area, capacity, and personal reference measures.

Numeration and Order Recognizing place value in numerals for whole numbers and decimals, expressing numbers in scientific notation; finding factors of numbers; comparing properties of prime and composite numbers; representing rates and ratios with fraction notation.

Operations Extending whole-number facts with addition, subtraction, multiplication, and division; evaluating symbolic expressions.

Patterns, Functions, and Sequences Determining divisibility; exploring number patterns; applying formulas to geometric figures.

Reference Frames Locating items with reference to an origin or zero point; for example, ordinal numbers, times of day, dates, and temperatures.

Throughout the year you will receive Parent Letters to keep you informed of the mathematical content studied in each of the units. Letters may include definitions of new terms as well as suggestions for at-home activities designed to reinforce skills.

We are looking forward to an exciting year filled with discovery and understanding. You will enjoy seeing your child's mathematical understanding grow.

© 1999 Everyday Learning Corporation

Study Link 9: Review

1. Fill in the missing numbers.

   a. $8^2 =$ _____   **b.** _____ $^2 = 64$ **c.** $3^2 =$ _____

   d. What is the square root of 36? _____

2. **a.** Name a number between 30 and
      45 that is divisible by 7, but not by 6.   _____

   b. Name a number between 500 and
      600 that is divisible by 5, but not by 10. _____

3. **a.** Circle the correct prime factorization of 45.

      $5 * 9$ $2 * 3 * 3 * 5$ $2 * 2 * 2 * 5$ $3 * 3 * 5$

   b. What is the longest factor string for 80? _____

4. Give an example of the following:

   a. An even number _____   **b.** A composite number _____

   c. An odd number _____   **d.** A square number _____

   e. A prime number _____   **f.** A multiple of 8 _____

5. **a.** List all the factors of 28. _____

   b. List all the factors of 36. _____

6. Theresa said, "If I square my little sister's age,
   I get my dad's age." If Theresa's dad is older
   than 25 and younger than 50, how old could
   Theresa's little sister be?   _____

7. Sally said, "I know that 15 is a prime number because I can make an array
   with only one row." • • • • • • • • • • • • • • Explain why she is wrong.

   _____

   _____

   _____

   _____

Array Dot Paper

Study Link 11: Estimating Measurements

For each statement below, mark whether the measurement given is…

S: too small **OK:** reasonable **L:** too large

_____ **1.** The width of the teacher's desk is 5 yards.

_____ **2.** A paper clip weighs about 3 kilograms.

_____ **3.** The length of an adult's step is about 1.5 feet.

_____ **4.** The distance between New York City and Los Angeles is about 670 miles.

_____ **5.** The length of a popsicle stick is about 10 centimeters.

_____ **6.** A full bathtub holds about 50 cups of water.

_____ **7.** The diameter of a penny is about 7 inches.

_____ **8.** It would take about 2.5 minutes to walk a mile.

_____ **9.** The temperature in Chicago during the summer is about 84°F.

_____ **10.** Most people like to drink their soft drinks at a temperature of about 0°C.

How Salty Is Seawater?

On average, seawater is 3.3% to 3.7% salt. Bodies of water such as the Persian Gulf and the Red Sea have salt contents over 4.2%. The Dead Sea is called "dead" because it is 25% salt and nothing can live in it. If all the salt in the oceans were removed and dried, it would form a mass of solid salt the size of Africa.

Source: _The Handy Science Answer Book._

Study Link 12: Number Hunt

Reminder: Whenever you see a on a page, this means that you are to solve the problems on that page without using a calculator. If there is no such symbol on the page, it means that you may use a calculator.

Use the numbers in the following table to answer the questions below. You may not use a number more than once.

19	85.2	533	571
88.2	525	20	17.5
400	261	20.5	125
7	23	901	30

1. Circle two numbers whose sum is 832.

2. Make an X in the boxes containing three numbers whose sum is 57.

3. Make a check mark in the boxes containing two prime numbers whose sum is 42.

4. Make a star in the boxes containing two numbers whose sum is 658.

5. Make a triangle in the boxes containing two numbers whose sum is 105.7.

The Six Smallest Countries

Country	Area (sq mi)	Population	Location
Vatican City	0.2	750	Rome, Italy
Monaco	0.6	28,000	French Riviera
Nauru	8	8,000	Western Pacific
Tuvalu	10	7,500	West Central Pacific
San Marino	24	19,000	North Central Italy
Liechtenstein	61	27,000	Between Switzerland and Austria

Did You Know?

Study Link 13: Another Number Hunt

Use the numbers in the following table to answer the questions below.
You may not use a number more than once.

17	15	9	75.03
100.9	803	25	451
1500	5000	1	3096
299	703	75.3	40.03

1. Circle two numbers whose difference is 152.

2. Make an X in the boxes of two numbers whose difference is 25.6.

3. Make a check mark in the boxes of two numbers whose difference is greater than 1000.

4. Make a star in the boxes of two numbers whose difference is less than 10.

5. Make a triangle in the boxes of two numbers whose difference is equal to the sum of 538 and 259.

6. Make a smiley face in the boxes of two numbers whose difference is equal to 4^2.

Population

Earth's population is growing by more than 200,000 people per day or about 80 million people per year. According to one projection, the rate of growth might increase to nearly 1 billion people per decade. In another projection, the rate of growth slows to about 600 million people per decade.

Source: *World Population Prospects, 1950–2050.*

Study Link 14: Driving Decimals

The table at the right shows the ten fastest winning speeds for the Indianapolis 500, a car race held each year at the Indianapolis Motor Speedway. The racers drive over 200 laps on a $2\frac{1}{2}$-mile oval. As of 1997, Rick Mears had won more prize money than any other driver—$4,299,392.

Driver	Year	Speed (mph)
Arie Luyendyk	1990	185.981
Rick Mears	1991	176.457
Bobby Rahal	1986	170.722
Emerson Fittipaldi	1989	167.581
Rick Mears	1984	163.612
Mark Donohue	1972	162.962
Al Unser	1987	162.175
Tom Sneva	1983	162.117
Gordon Johncock	1982	162.029
Al Unser	1978	161.363

1. a. What was Emerson Fittipaldi's winning speed for the Indianapolis 500?

   _____
   unit

   b. In what year did he set this speed record?

   _____

2. How much faster was Rick Mears's speed in 1991 than in 1984?

   _____
   unit

3. What is the range of speeds in the table?

   Reminder: The range is the difference between the fastest speed and the slowest speed.

   _____
   unit

4. a. Which two drivers have the smallest difference between their winning speeds?

   _____

   b. What is the difference between the two speeds?

   _____
   unit

Challenge

5. What is the median of the speeds in the table? _____
   unit

Source: Indianapolis Motor Speedway Internet Site–http://www.indyracingleague.com/ims/index.html

Study Link 17: Which Is Largest?

Which of the following problems has the largest answer?
Try to figure it out by solving as few problems as possible.
Record the largest answer.

1. $52 * 31 =$ _____

2. $6351 + 2860 =$ _____

3.   _____ $= 80 * 93$

4. $96.76 - 5.30 =$ _____

5. $4356 + 147 =$ _____

6. $3 * 2649 =$ _____

7.   _____ $= 9115 - 127$

8.   _____ $= 999.9 + 99.9$

Old Math

The ancient Egyptians used picture symbols, called hieroglyphs, to record numbers.

Here is how the Egyptians solved $11 * 13$. Can you figure out how they did it?

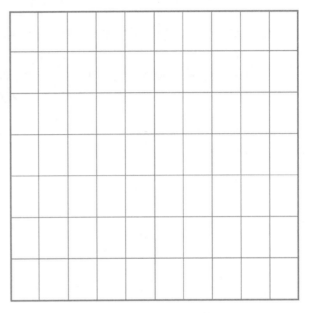

Study Link 18: Estimation

1. Use only estimation to answer the following questions.

   a. Certain varieties of sea horses can move 10.5 inches per minute. Would these sea horses be able to travel 6 yards in 1 hour? _____

   b. Orville Wright completed the first successful airplane flight on December 17, 1903. He traveled 120 feet in 12 seconds. If he had been able to stay in the air for a full minute, would he have traveled 1 mile? (*Hint:* 1 mile = 5280 feet) _____

   c. In 1960, the *Triton* became the first submarine to circumnavigate the world. It covered 36,014 miles in 76 days. Is that more or less than 100 miles per day? _____

2. It is said that the Aztec king, Montezuma, drank about 50 cups of chocolate a day. Based on this information, answer the following questions.

   About how much did he drink per week? _____
                                                                    unit

   About how much per year? _____
                                                      unit

   Source: *The Kids' World Almanac of Records and Facts.*

Challenge

3. The second edition of the *Oxford English Dictionary* was published, in 20 volumes, in 1989. The dictionary contains entries for 557,889 words. The three letters with the fewest word entries are *X* with 152 entries, *Z* with 733 entries, and *Q* with 1824 entries. The letter *S* has the most entries—34,556. How many more entries does the letter *S* have than the combined total of the letters *X, Z,* and *Q*? _____
                                                          unit

4. In 1992, President Clinton earned a salary of about $550 per day as President. That same year, Bill Cosby earned an average of about $180,000 per day. On an average, about how much more did Bill Cosby earn in a week than President Clinton? _____
                                                          unit

   Source: *The Top 10 of Everything.*

Study Link 3: Factors

Here is one way to find all the factors of 15. Ask yourself:

	Yes/No	Number Sentence	Factor Pair
Is 1 a factor of 15?	Yes	1 * 15 = 15	1, 15
Is 2 a factor of 15?	No		
Is 3 a factor of 15?	Yes	3 * 5 = 15	3, 5
Is 4 a factor of 15?	No		

You don't need to go any further. Can you tell why? _____

_____

_____

_____

The factors of 15 are 1, 3, 5, and 15.

List as many factors as you can for each of the following numbers.

1. 25 _____

2. 28 _____

3. 40 _____

4. 42 _____

5. 48 _____

Challenge

6. 64 _____

7. 100 _____

Study Link 4: Divisibility Tests

- All even numbers are **divisible by 2.**
- A number is **divisible by 10** if it ends in 0.
- A number is **divisible by 3** if the sum of its digits is divisible by 3.
- A number is **divisible by 6** if it is divisible both by 2 and by 3.
- A number is **divisible by 9** if the sum of its digits is divisible by 9.
- A number is **divisible by 5** if it ends in 0 or 5.

1. Use divisibility tests to check whether the following numbers are divisible by 2, 3, 5, 6, 9, or 10.

Number	Divisible by:					
	2	**3**	**5**	**6**	**9**	**10**
998,876						
5,890						
72,344						
36,540						
861						
33,015						
1,098						
45,369						
4,009,721						

A number is divisible by 4 if the tens and ones digits form a number that is divisible by 4. For example: 47,**836** is divisible by 4, because 36 is divisible by 4.

It isn't always easy to tell whether the last two digits form a number that is divisible by 4. A quick way to check is to divide the number by 2 and then divide the result by 2. This is the same as dividing by 4, but it is often easier to do mentally. For example: 5,**384** is divisible by 4, because 84 / 2 = 42 and 42 / 2 = 21. And: The number 9**67** is not divisible by 4, because 67 / 2 = $33\frac{1}{2}$.

Challenge

2. Put a star next to any number in the table that is divisible by 4.

Study Link 6: Number Patterns

Draw the dot pattern that comes next and record the number of dots in the pattern.

Example:

1.

2.

3.

4.

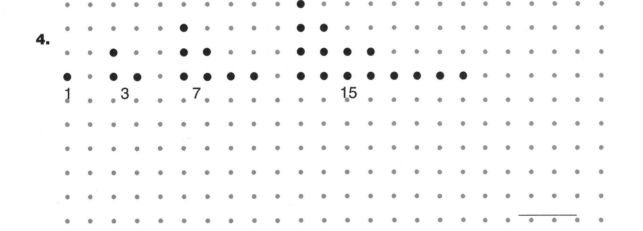

Use with Lesson 6.   **Unit 1**

Study Link 5: Prime and Composite Numbers

A **prime number** is a whole number that has exactly two factors—1 and the number itself. A **composite number** is a whole number that has more than two factors.

1. Tell whether the following numbers are **prime** or **composite.**

   a. The number of quarts in a gallon   _____

   b. The number of months in a year   _____

   c. The number of days in a week   _____

   d. The number of sides in a hexagon   _____

   e. The number of sides in a pentagon   _____

2. Write each of the following numbers as the sum of two **prime** numbers.

   Examples: 56 = **43 + 13**   26 = **13 + 13**

   a.   6 = _____   **b.**   12 = _____

   c.   18 = _____   **d.**   22 = _____

   e.   24 = _____   **f.**   34 = _____

3. Can any of the numbers in Part 2 be written as the sum of two prime numbers in more than one way? If so, give an example. _____

   _____

   ┌──┐
   │ The answers to these problems are examples of **Goldbach's Conjecture,**
   │ which states that every even number greater than 2 can be named
   │ as a sum of two primes. No one has been able to find an even number
   │ greater than 2 that cannot be expressed as a sum of two prime numbers.
   │ Neither has anyone been able to prove that this conjecture is true for all
   │ such numbers. Anyone who can either prove or disprove Goldbach's
   │ Conjecture will become famous.
   └──┘

Challenge

4. Write 70 as the sum of two primes. _____

_____

Study Link 8: Prime Factorization

You may remember that a square number can be written as the product of a number multiplied by itself. This is called **exponential notation.** For example, 5 ∗ 5 can be written as 5^2. The raised 2 is called the **exponent**—it tells how many times 5 is used as a factor.

You can use exponential notation to write a product where a factor is used more than two times. For example: $5^3 = 5 ∗ 5 ∗ 5$. It may be read as "5 cubed" or as "5 to the third power." And: $7^4 = 7 ∗ 7 ∗ 7 ∗ 7$ is read as "7 to the fourth power."

When a number is written as a product of whole numbers other than 1, we call this a factor string. For example, 2 ∗ 3 ∗ 6 is a factor string for 36.

The longest factor string for a number is called its **prime factorization** because it is made of prime numbers only. The prime factorization of 36 is 2 ∗ 2 ∗ 3 ∗ 3. The prime factorization of a number can be written using exponential notation: $36 = 2^2 ∗ 3^2$.

1. Write each of the following numbers written in exponential notation as a product of factors. Then use your calculator to find the answer.

   a. $2^3 ∗ 3 =$ _____ *2 ∗ 2 ∗ 2 ∗ 3* _____ = _____ *24* _____

   b. $2 ∗ 3^3 ∗ 5^2 =$ _____ = _____

   c. $5^4 =$ _____ = _____

   d. $2^6 ∗ 4^2 =$ _____ = _____

2. Write each number below as a product of factors. Then write it in exponential notation.

   a. 12 = _____ *2 ∗ 2 ∗ 3* _____ = _____ $2^2 ∗ 3$ _____

   b. 36 = _____ = _____

   c. 32 = _____ = _____

   d. 90 = _____ = _____

Study Link 7: Factor Rainbows

1. List all the factors of each of the first 10 square numbers. Make a factor rainbow to check your work. **Reminder:** In a factor rainbow, the product of each connected factor pair should be equal to the number itself. For example, the factor rainbow for the number 4 looks like this:

1 2 4 $1 * 4 = 4$ $2 * 2 = 4$

1:	36:
4:	49:
9:	64:
16:	81:
25:	100:

2. Do all square numbers have an odd number of factors? _____

   If no, which square number(s) in Part 1
   above have an even number of factors? _____

3. Which square numbers in Part 1 have exactly 3 factors? _____

   What do they have in common? _____

   _____

   _____

Study Link: Parent Letter

Unit 1: Number Theory

The mathematics program we are using this year—*Everyday Mathematics*—will prepare students to make sound decisions in areas that involve mathematics. The students will have many experiences to help them form an appreciation of the many ways mathematics affects our daily lives.

During the next 2 or 3 weeks, our class will study properties of whole numbers. Students will first look at very concrete representations of numbers, called **rectangular arrays.** These arrays are arrangements of objects into rows and columns, with equal numbers of objects in each row and column.

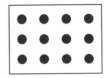

A 3-by-4 array

Your child will use arrays to find the **factor pairs** for whole numbers. When the numbers in a factor pair for a number n are multiplied, the result is the number n. For example, 3 and 4 are a factor pair for 12 because $3 \times 4 = 12$. The numbers 3 and 4 are both **factors** of 12. This can be seen in the array for 12 shown above—it has 3 rows of dots with 4 dots in each row. The other factor pairs of 12 are 2 and 6 (since $2 \times 6 = 12$), and 1 and 12 (since $1 \times 12 = 12$).

Arrays and factor pairs form the basis for many of the topics in Unit 1.

- Numbers, such as 9 and 16, which can be represented by square arrays—arrays with the same number of dots in all rows and columns—are called **square numbers.**

A square array

- Numbers, such as 6 and 10, which can be represented by arrays of 2 rows (or 2 columns) are called **even numbers.** Numbers, such as 3 and 15, which cannot be represented in this way are called **odd numbers.**

- Numbers, such as 5 and 11, which have exactly one factor pair each are called **prime numbers.** Numbers, such as 8 and 12, which have more than two factors each are called **composite numbers.**

A quick way to find out whether a number m is a factor of a number n is to check whether n is **divisible by** m. For example, 12 is divisible by 4; therefore, 4 is a factor of 12. The class will learn several shortcuts to check whether a number is divisible by another number, without actually having to carry out the division.

To practice finding factors of whole numbers, the class will learn to play the game *Factor Captor,* which combines skill in finding factors of numbers with strategic thinking. Ask your child to show you how to play the game.

In Unit 1, students will be asked to collect pictures of arrays to form a class Arrays Museum. Pictures may include objects such as floor tiles, windows, and checkerboards. You may want to help your child find pictures to contribute. To practice using arrays with your child at home, use any small objects, such as beans, macaroni, or pennies.

Finally, you may want to help your child memorize the basic multiplication facts found in the multiplication table. You can work together using the Fact Triangles, or you may play *Beat the Calculator, Multiplication Top-It,* or *Baseball Multiplication.* These are games that were introduced in previous grades of *Everyday Mathematics.*

This should be a stimulating year. We invite you to share the excitement with us.

Study Link 2: Two-Row Arrays

1. Make a 14-dot array that has exactly 2 rows.

    How many dots are in each row? _____

2. Some of the following numbers can be arranged into 2-row arrays. The other numbers cannot.

    9   16   2   15   20   33

    a. Which of the numbers can be arranged into 2-row arrays?

        _____

    b. Draw a 2-row array for each number in Part a.

    c. List all the numbers up to 20 that can be arranged into 2-row arrays.

        _____

        _____

    d. What do we call the numbers in Part c?

        _____

    e. What do we call numbers that cannot be arranged into 2-row arrays?

        _____

Reminder

Look for examples of arrays and bring them to school.

Multiplication Facts

A List					
3 * 6 = 18					
6 * 3 = 18					
3 * 7 = 21					
7 * 3 = 21					
3 * 8 = 24					
8 * 3 = 24					
3 * 9 = 27					
9 * 3 = 27					
4 * 6 = 24					
6 * 4 = 24					
4 * 7 = 28					
7 * 4 = 28					
4 * 8 = 32					
8 * 4 = 32					
4 * 9 = 36					
9 * 4 = 36					
5 * 7 = 35					
7 * 5 = 35					
5 * 9 = 45					
9 * 5 = 45					
6 * 6 = 36					
6 * 7 = 42					
7 * 6 = 42					
6 * 8 = 48					
8 * 6 = 48					
6 * 9 = 54					
9 * 6 = 54					
7 * 7 = 49					
7 * 8 = 56					
8 * 7 = 56					
7 * 9 = 63					
9 * 7 = 63					
8 * 8 = 64					
8 * 9 = 72					
9 * 8 = 72					
9 * 9 = 81					

B List					
3 * 3 = 9					
3 * 4 = 12					
4 * 3 = 12					
3 * 5 = 15					
5 * 3 = 15					
4 * 4 = 16					
4 * 5 = 20					
5 * 4 = 20					
5 * 5 = 25					
5 * 6 = 30					
6 * 5 = 30					
5 * 8 = 40					
8 * 5 = 40					
6 * 10 = 60					
10 * 6 = 60					
7 * 10 = 70					
10 * 7 = 70					
8 * 10 = 80					
10 * 8 = 80					
9 * 10 = 90					
10 * 9 = 90					
10 * 10 = 100					

Bonus Problems					
11 * 11 = 121					
11 * 12 = 132					
5 * 12 = 60					
12 * 6 = 72					
7 * 12 = 84					
12 * 8 = 96					
9 * 12 = 108					
10 * 12 = 120					
5 * 13 = 65					
15 * 7 = 105					
12 * 12 = 144					
6 * 14 = 84					

Use with Lesson 2 and following.

✔ Checking Progress

1. Mr. Martin has 24 tulip bulbs. He wants to plant them in a rectangular array consisting of at least 2 rows with at least 2 tulips in each row. On the grid at the right, draw 3 possible arrays.

2. a. Is 24 an even or an odd number?

    _____

    b. Is 24 a prime or a composite number?

    _____

    Explain why.

    _____

    _____

    _____

    _____

    c. List all the factors of 24. _____

3. Fill in the missing numbers.

    a. $7^2 =$ _____   b. $9^2 =$ _____

    c. $25^2 =$ _____   d. _____$^2 = 100$

    e. What is the square root of 25? _____

4. Circle the correct prime factorization of 30.

    2 * 3 * 4 * 5   2 * 3 * 5   3 * 3 * 3 * 3   2 * 3 * 10

5. What is the longest factor string for 50? _____

✔ Checking Progress (continued)

6. Pretend that you are playing *Factor Captor* on the number grid at the right. The crossed-out numbers have already been picked.

✗1	2	✗3	4	✗5
6	✗7	8	9	10
11	12	13	14	15
16	17	18	19	20
✗21	22	✗23	24	✗25
26	27	28	✗29	30

a. Which number would you choose next?

_____

Why?

_____

_____

_____

b. If you chose 24, how many points would your opponent be able to score? _____

7. a. Name a number between 200 and 300 that is divisible by 3 but not by 2. _____

b. Name a number between 200 and 300 that is divisible by 2, 3, and 5. _____

8. At the right is a calendar for a month. Use the following clues to figure out on what date the Bret Harte School won its last basketball game.

S	M	T	W	T	F	S
	1	2	3	4	5	6
7	8	9	10	11	12	13
14	15	16	17	18	19	20
21	22	23	24	25	26	27
28	29	30	31			

• The date is not an even number.

• It is not a square number.

• It is not a prime number.

• It is a multiple of 5.

On what day of the month did the school win its last basketball game? _____

9. Is 231 a prime or composite number?

Explain your answer.

_____

_____

✔ Checking Progress (continued)

5. Mrs. Ramirez earns $95 per day. How much
   does she earn in a 5-day work week? _____

6. Caitlin's great-grandmother was born in 1908.
   Her family had a big party for her on her 85th birthday.
   In what year did they have the party? _____

7. Each section of the stadium has 15 rows. There
   are 26 seats in each row. How many seats are
   there in each section of the stadium? _____

8. Normally, Seth's body temperature is 98.6°F.
   This morning, he woke up with a fever of 102.4°F.
   By noon, his temperature had gone down 1.7
   degrees. How many degrees above normal was
   Seth's temperature at noon? _____

9. Michael and Tanika are in charge of ordering pizzas for their class party.
   There are 22 students in their class.

   • A large cheese pizza serves about 6 people and costs $11.45.

   • An extra-large cheese pizza serves about 8 people and costs $13.75.

   • Each extra ingredient costs $0.50 on a large pizza and $0.75 on
     an extra-large pizza.

Use this information to make up a number story. Then solve it.

Number story: _____

_____

_____

_____

Answer: _____

What I did: _____

_____

_____

_____

Unit 2

Estimation & Calculation

Study Link: Parent Letter

Unit 2: Estimation and Calculation

Computation is an important part of problem solving. Fortunately, we are no longer restricted to paper-and-pencil methods of computation. We can use a calculator to solve lengthy problems or even a computer program to solve very complex ones. Throughout the year, students will have many opportunities to practice estimation, mental, and paper-and-pencil methods of computation; to use a calculator; and to decide which method is most appropriate for solving a particular problem.

Unit 2 focuses primarily on different methods for paper-and-pencil computation. Many of us were taught that there is just one way to do each kind of computation. For example, we may have learned to subtract by "borrowing," without realizing that there are many other methods of subtracting numbers.

While students will not be expected to learn more than one method for performing each of the four basic operations (addition, subtraction, multiplication, and division), the authors of *Everyday Mathematics* want them to examine several different methods and to realize that there are often several ways to accomplish the same task and achieve the same result. The authors also want students to have the option of learning the methods they find most comfortable, or even inventing methods of their own. Encourage your child to share some of these new methods with you.

The class will also work on the first **Estimation Challenge** of the year. This is a problem for which it is very difficult, time consuming, and perhaps even impossible to find an exact answer. Students work with partners or in small groups to come up with and defend their best estimates. Estimation Challenges will be presented several times during the school year.

Your child will also learn a new game—*Multiplication Bull's-eye*—that provides practice with estimation. You might want to play this game with your child at home. Instructions could be found on *Journal 1,* page 58.

✔ Checking Progress

1. On the numeral at the right   406,275.02

   a. draw a line under the digit in the tens place.

   b. cross out the digit in the hundredths place.

   c. draw a circle around the digit in the thousands place.

   d. draw a line over the digit in the hundred-thousands place.

2. Solve each of these problems by any method you choose.
Show your work on the computation grid below.

   a. $167 + 285 =$ _____   **b.** _____ $= 459 - 237$

   c. $549 + 130 + 37 =$ _____   **d.** $4.07 - 1.85 =$ _____

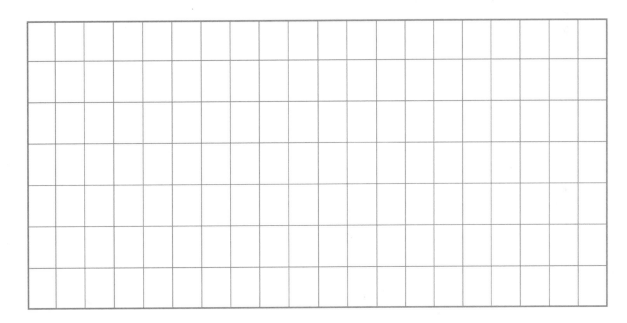

3. Jenny bowled five games in the tournament.
Her scores were 79, 102, 86, 115, and 98.

   a. What was her maximum score? _____

   b. What was her minimum score? _____

   c. What was the range of her scores? _____

   d. What was her median score? _____

✔ Checking Progress (continued)

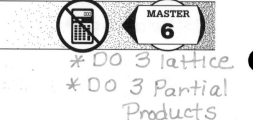

*DO 3 lattice
*DO 3 Partial
   Products

4. Solve each problem below·
    Show your work on the computation grid.

   a. _____ = 6 * 38   **b.**   24 * 30 = _____

   c.   108 * 9 = _____   **d.**   47 * 35 = _____

   e. _____ = 50 * 720   **f.** 241 * 16 = _____

Unit 3

Geometry

Explorations

&

the American

Tour

Study Link: Parent Letter

Unit 3: Geometry Explorations and the American Tour

In Unit 3 your child will set out on the American Tour, a yearlong series of mathematical activities that will examine historical, demographic, and environmental features of the United States. The American Tour involves a wide range of mathematical skills, but most importantly it seeks to develop your child's ability to read, interpret, critically examine, and use mathematical information presented in text, tables, and graphics. These skills are essential to effective mathematics in our technological age.

Many American Tour activities are based on materials in the *American Tour Almanac,* a reference book specially designed for the *Everyday Mathematics* curriculum. The *American Tour Almanac,* a cross between an historical atlas and an almanac, contains maps, data, and other information from a wide range of sources, including the U.S. Census Bureau, the National Weather Service, and the National Geographic Society. Please note that students do not write in this book.

Unit 3 also will review some geometry concepts from earlier grades, while introducing and expanding on others. In *Fourth Grade Everyday Mathematics,* students used a compass to construct basic shapes and create geometric designs. In this unit, your child will extend these skills and will be introduced to the concept of congruent figures (same size, same shape) by using a compass and straightedge to copy triangles. Another tool that will be introduced is the Geometry Template, which contains protractors and rulers for measuring and cutouts for drawing a variety of geometric figures.

Finally, the students will be introduced to the mathematics and art of tessellations—patterns of shapes that cover a surface without gaps or overlaps—and will begin to create their own designs.

You may wish to help your child at home by asking questions about information presented in newspaper and magazine tables and graphics. Also, our world is filled with many 2-dimensional and 3-dimensional geometric forms: angles, line segments, curves, cubes, cylinders, spheres, pyramids, and so on. Many wonderful geometric patterns can be seen in nature as well as in the things that people create. It will be helpful for you and your child to look for and talk about geometric shapes throughout the year.

Study Link 20: A Mental Calculation Strategy

When a number being multiplied ends in 9, you can simplify the calculation by changing it into an easier problem. Then you adjust the result.

Example: $2 * 99 = ?$

1. Change $2 * 99$ into $2 * 100$.

2. Find the answer: $2 * 100 = 200$.

3. Ask, "How is the answer to $2 * 100$ different from the answer to $2 * 99$?" Since 100 is 1 more than 99, and you multiplied by 2, 200 is 2 more than the answer to $2 * 99$.

4. Adjust the answer to $2 * 100$ to find the answer to $2 * 99$: $200 - 2 = 198$. So $2 * 99 = 198$.

This strategy also works for numbers ending in 7 or 8.

Example: $5 * 48$

1. Change $5 * 48$ into $5 * 50$.

2. Find the answer: $5 * 50 = 250$.

3. Ask, "How is $5 * 50$ different from $5 * 48$?"
50 is 2 more than 48, and you multiplied by 5.
So 250 is $5 * 2$, or 10, more than the answer to $5 * 48$.

4. Adjust: $250 - 10 = 240$. So $5 * 48 = 240$.

Use this strategy. Try to calculate the following in your head.

1. $4 * 99 =$ _____

2. $2 * 48 =$ _____

3. $6 * 39 =$ _____

4. $3 * 97 =$ _____

5. $3 * 399 =$ _____

6. $6 * 98 =$ _____

7. $5 * 249 =$ _____

8. $5 * 198 =$ _____

Study Link 21: Distance to School

There are two ways to get from Josephina's house to school. She can take Elm Street to Washington Avenue. She can also take Snakey Lane.

Use the map and scale below to answer the questions.

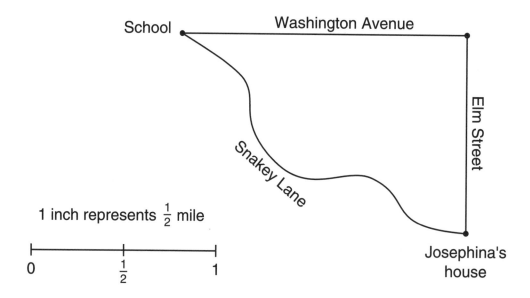

1 inch represents $\frac{1}{2}$ mile

1. Josephina started walking along Elm Street.

   a. How far would Josephina walk before she turned onto Washington Avenue? _____

   b. How far would she be from school when she turned the corner? _____

2. **a.** If Josephina wants to take the shortest route to school, which road(s) should she take? _____

   b. What is this distance? _____

3. Josephina's father jogged to the school along Snakey Lane and then back along Washington Avenue and Elm Street to his house. About how far did he jog in all? _____

4. Josephina left school and walked down Snakey Lane. Her father left home at the same time and walked up Snakey Lane. If her father was walking twice as fast as Josephina, where did they meet? Put a mark on the road where they met.

Study Link 22: The Constitutional Convention

After the United States declared its independence from Great Britain, the new nation was governed under a document called the **Articles of Confederation.** The Articles of Confederation did not work well. For one thing, the national government did not have the power to tax the people. It had to rely on the states to contribute money—and the states had a great deal of difficulty collecting from the citizens.

Leaders such as Alexander Hamilton and James Madison urged that a meeting be held to change the Articles of Confederation. This meeting, which was eventually called the Constitutional Convention, was held in Philadelphia, Pennsylvania, in 1787. The delegates had much to debate and decide. In about four months, they produced a new document, the **Constitution of the United States.** The United States has been governed under the Constitution (with some additions and changes) since 1789.

George Washington was elected chairman of the Constitutional Convention. He wrote that the delegates met for "not less than five, and for a large part of the time six, and sometimes seven hours sitting every day, except Sundays and the ten days' adjournment [break]."

The Constitutional Convention began on Friday, May 25, 1787, and ended on Monday, September 17, 1787.

1. Estimate the number of days the delegates met to work on the Constitution. _____

2. Use Washington's figures to estimate the number of hours they met. _____

More about the Constitutional Convention

- In 1787, Philadelphia was the country's largest city. Its population was 45,000.

- The Constitutional Convention was held in the Old State House (now called Independence Hall), in the room where the Declaration of Independence was signed in 1776. Meetings were not open to the public.

- Nine states were required to ratify (approve) the Constitution. The ninth state was New Hampshire, which ratified it on June 21, 1788. The last of the original thirteen states to ratify the Constitution was Rhode Island, in 1790.

Study Link 23: Angle Measures

1. What is the measure of each angle below?

   a. measure of ∠CAT = _____°

   b. measure of ∠BAR = _____°

   c. measure of ∠RAT = _____°

   d. measure of ∠CAB = _____°

   e. measure of ∠BAT = _____°

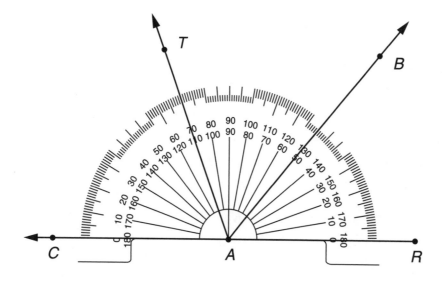

2. What is the measure of each angle at the right?

   a. measure of ∠MEN = _____°

   b. measure of ∠DEN = _____°

   c. measure of ∠MET = _____°

   d. measure of ∠MED = _____°

   e. measure of ∠TEN = _____°

   f. measure of ∠TED = _____°

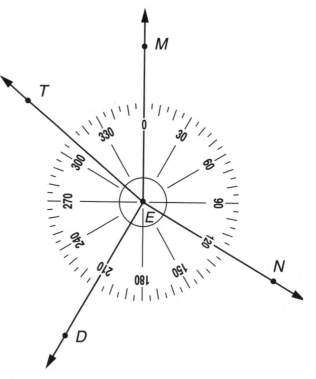

Study Link 24: Baseball Angles

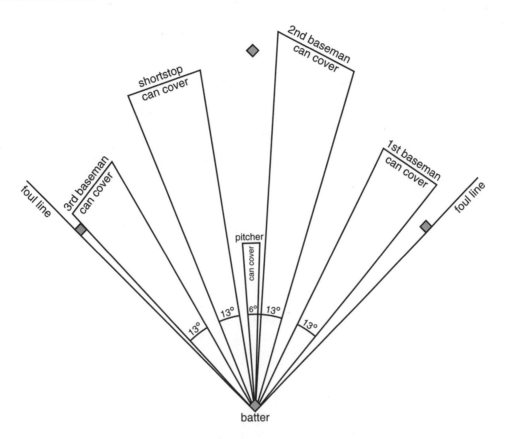

The playing field for baseball lies between the foul lines, which form a 90°
angle. Suppose that each of the four infielders can cover an angle of about 13°
on a hard-hit ground ball, and that the pitcher can cover about 6°. (See the
diagram above.)

1. How many degrees are left for the batter to hit through? _____

    Source: *Applying Arithmetic.*

2. Look up the word *acute* in a dictionary. Write at least one meaning of the
    word in addition to the one you know in mathematics.

    _____

    _____

3. Look up the word *obtuse.* Write at least one other meaning in addition to the
    one you know in mathematics.

    _____

    _____

Study Link 25: Angles and Patterns

1. Use what you know about vertical and adjacent angles to fill in the missing angle measures below.

a.

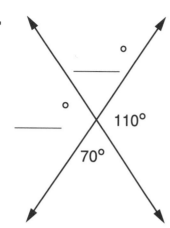

b.

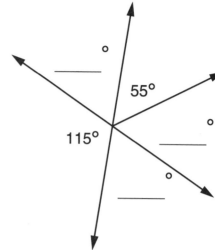

2. Continue each of the following patterns.

a.

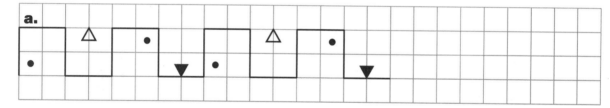

b.

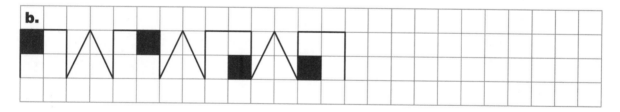

c.

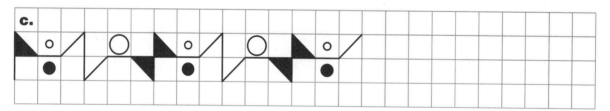

3. Draw a pattern of your own in the grid below.

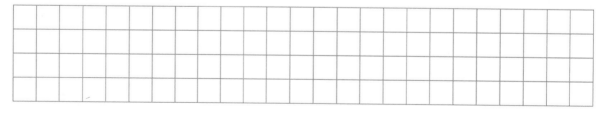

Study Link 26: Geometry Puzzles

1. Look at each row below. Which of the three pictures on the right shows what the paper on the left will look like when you unfold it? Circle the best answer.

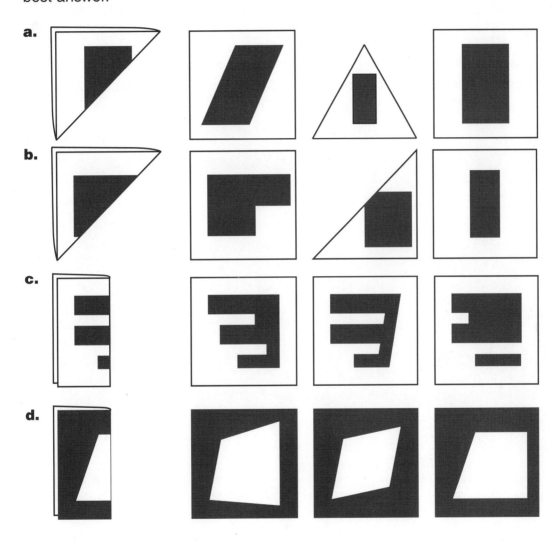

a.

b.

c.

d.

2. If the paper on the left is unfolded and then turned 90° clockwise, which of the three pictures on the right will it look like? Circle the best answer.

Study Link 27: Tessellations Museum

Collect examples of tessellations. Look in newspapers and magazines. Ask people at home to help you find examples.

Ask an adult if you may cut the tessellations out. If you may, tape them onto this page.

If you are not able to find examples in newspapers and magazines, try looking around your home on the furniture and wallpaper. Then, in the space below, sketch the tessellations that you are able to find.

Study Link 28: The Sums of Angle Measures

1. Draw a large triangle on a separate sheet of paper using a straightedge. Draw an arc in each angle. Then cut out the triangle and tear off part of each angle (see example below). Tape or glue the angles on the back of the page so that pairs of angles touch but do not overlap.

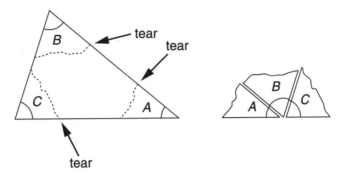

It appears that the sum of the
measures of the angles of any triangle is _____ °.

2. Draw a large quadrangle on a separate sheet of paper using a straightedge. Draw an arc in each angle. Cut out the quadrangle and tear off part of each angle (see example below). Tape or glue the angles on the back of the page so that pairs of angles touch but do not overlap.

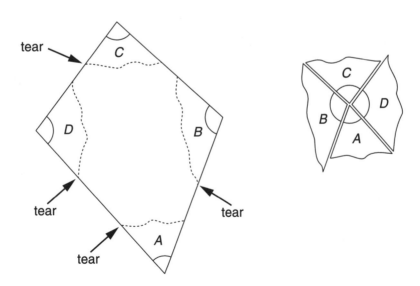

It appears that the sum of the
measures of the angles of any quadrangle is _____ °.

Study Link 29: Polygons and Their Measures

1. Draw each of the following figures on the back of this page.

    a. a polygon   **b.** a triangle with no equal sides

    c. a quadrangle with one   **d.** a quadrangle with no pairs of
        right angle   parallel sides

2. Without using a protractor, record the missing angle measurements in the figure below.

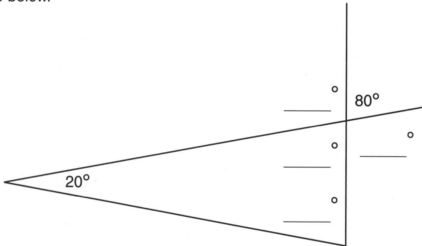

3. Use the following figure to answer the following questions.

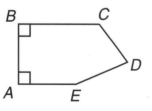

    a. How long is line segment *CD*?   _____

    b. What is the measure of angle *A*?   _____

    c. Which angle in the figure has the smallest measure?   _____

    d. What is a geometric name for the figure?   _____

✔ Cumulative Review

MASTER 8

1. A parking lot has 7 rows. Each row has spaces for 9 cars. How many cars can be parked in this lot? _____

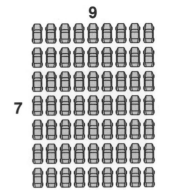

2. A section of the school auditorium has 9 rows. Each row has 35 seats. How many people can be seated in this section? _____

3. Circle the prime factorization of 20.

$$3 * 5 * 5 \qquad 2 * 3 * 4 * 5 \qquad 2 * 3 * 5 \qquad 2 * 2 * 5$$

4. According to the U.S. Census, the population in 1790 was three million, nine hundred twenty-nine thousand, two hundred fourteen.

    a. Write this number with digits. _____

    b. Is this number closer to 3 million or to 4 million? Explain.

_____

_____

_____

5. On the numeral at the right:

419.13

    a. Circle the digit in the tenths place.

    b. Underline the digit in the hundreds place.

    c. Cross out the digit whose value is 10.

    d. If you add 6 to the number above, the new number you get is _____.

6. 1275 + 246 = _____   **7.** 252 − 175 = _____

✱✱ *Do these partial.*

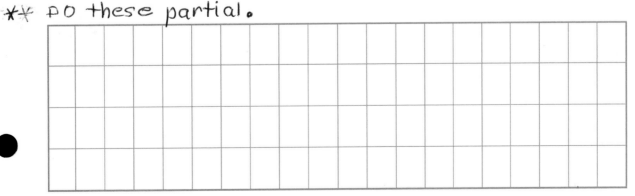

✔ Checking Progess

Name _____   Name _____

Name _____   Name _____

Group Assessment

1. Which of the following figures can be drawn? Circle the description if it can be drawn. Cross it out if it cannot be drawn. Try drawing the figures if you aren't sure.

   a. a triangle with two right angles   **b.** a triangle with an angle of 100°

   c. a rectangle with no sides equal   **d.** a quadrilateral with opposite sides parallel

2. Pick one figure in Problem 1 that you crossed out. Explain why it can't be drawn.

   _____

   _____

3. Find and record the missing angle measurements in the figure below.

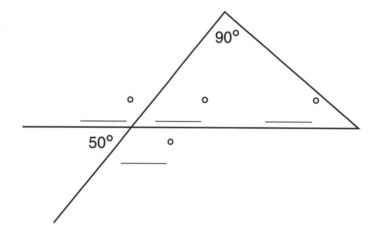

4. Josephina said that she could draw a parallelogram by putting two congruent (identical) triangles together. Use a triangle on your Geometry Template to show that this is true. Then use another triangle on the template and show that it is also true for that triangle. Show your work on the back of this page.

✔ Checking Progress

Individual Assessment

1. What kind of angle is formed by the lamppost and the ground?

_____

2. Find each figure described below on your Geometry Template. Use the template to draw each figure.

    a. a four-sided figure   **b.** a triangle with two sides of equal length

    c. a shape that is not a polygon   **d.** a polygon with opposite sides parallel and no right angles

3. Find and record the missing angle measurements in the figure below.

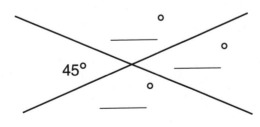

4. Below is a map of Lone Eagle State Beach. Use the map scale to answer the following questions to the nearest mile.

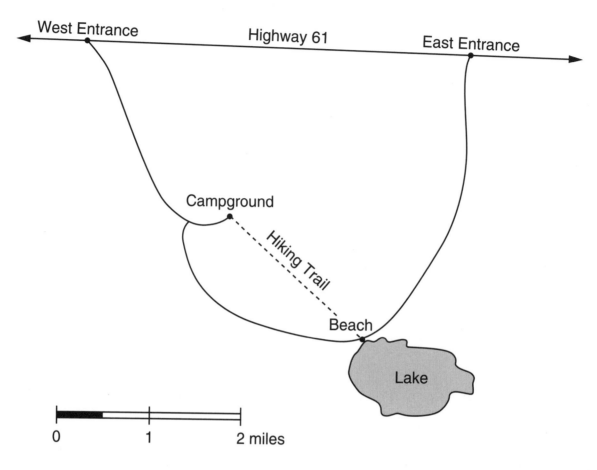

West Entrance   Highway 61   East Entrance

Campground

Hiking Trail

Beach

Lake

0   1   2 miles

a. How far apart are the East and West Entrances
of the park along Highway 61?   _____

b. Melissa and her family plan on hiking from the
campground to the beach. About how far will this
hike be if they take the road?   _____

c. How far will it be if they take the hiking trail?   _____

5.

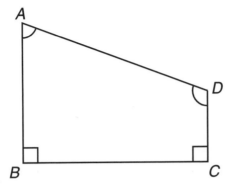

   a. How long is line segment *AD*? _____cm

   b. What is the measure of angle *B*? _____°

   c. Which angle in the figure has the largest measure? _____

      What is the measure of this angle? _____°

   d. What is a geometric name for the figure? _____

6. Use any geometry tools you wish. Copy the figure in Problem 5 in the space below.

Unit 4

Fractions, Decimals, & Percents

Study Link: Parent Letter

Unit 4: Fractions, Decimals, and Percents

The focus of Unit 4 will be on naming numbers as fractions, decimals, and percents. Your child will use pattern blocks to review basic fraction and mixed-number concepts and notations, and formulate rules for finding equivalent fractions.

In *Fourth Grade Everyday Mathematics,* your child learned to convert easy fractions, such as $\frac{1}{2}, \frac{1}{4}, \frac{1}{10}$, and $\frac{3}{4}$, to decimal and percent equivalencies. For example, the fraction $\frac{1}{2}$ can be renamed as 0.5 and as 50%. In this unit, students will learn (with the help of a calculator) how to rename **any** fraction as a decimal and as a percent.

In this unit, *Everyday Mathematics* introduces two new games: *Frac-Tac-Toe,* to practice converting fractions to decimals and percents, and *Estimation Squeeze,* to practice finding decimals between any two decimals. These games, like other games introduced earlier, are used to reduce the tedium that often comes with the drill and practice of arithmetic skills. Your child will look forward to playing these games. Both *Frac-Tac-Toe* and *Estimation Squeeze* use very simple materials so that you may play them at home.

Your child will also take part in the long-range project, "How Would You Spend a Million Dollars?" Your child will develop a plan for spending $1 million according to one particular theme such as building a new city park. Each child will find out what expenses will be incurred in carrying out the plan, keep an organized record of expenses, and report the results. Fraction, decimal, and percent equivalencies will be used in reporting these results, and circle graphs will be used to represent data.

Your child also will continue to explore historical, demographic, and environmental data about the United States. The class will study population information from various periods in U.S. history, using circle graphs and population distribution maps. This project will provide another opportunity to use fraction, decimal, and percent equivalencies.

Study Link 31: Addition and Subtraction Number Stories

1. After spending $1.83 for lunch, Jane has $2.27 left. How much money did she have before lunch? _____

2. One TV network allows a maximum of $9\frac{1}{2}$ minutes each hour for advertising and station breaks. How much time does that leave for program length? _____

3. John weighs 40 kg (kilograms). Marian weighs 32.5 kg. How much more than Marian does John weigh? _____

4. About 52% of adults wear glasses. About what percent of adults do not wear glasses? _____

5. A person works from 6:15 A.M. to 11:00 A.M. with a 15-minute break. How many hours of work is this? _____

6. A father weighed his 4-month-old baby this way: First, he stood on the scale without the baby, reading his weight as $154\frac{1}{4}$ pounds. Then he held the baby, and together baby and father weighed $170\frac{1}{2}$ pounds. How much did the baby weigh? _____

7. At the 1994 Winter Olympics, the U.S. bobsled team had four separate runs of 52.03 seconds, 52.42 seconds, 52.77 seconds, and 52.75 seconds. What was the combined time for all four runs? _____

Study Link 32: Fraction Practice

1. Find each of these lengths on the ruler shown below. Mark the ruler for each length. Write the letter above your mark. A and B are done for you.

A: 5" **B:** $\frac{1}{2}$" **C:** $3\frac{1}{2}$" **D:** $2\frac{1}{2}$"

E: $4\frac{3}{4}$" **F:** $\frac{1}{4}$" **G:** $4\frac{1}{8}$" **H:** $1\frac{7}{8}$"

I: $1\frac{3}{8}$" **J:** $\frac{15}{16}$" **K:** $3\frac{1}{16}$" **L:** $5\frac{9}{16}$"

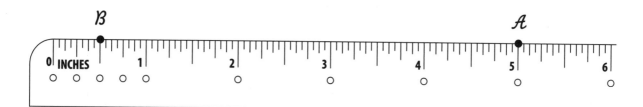

2. In the two figures below, write the correct fraction name in each of the smaller regions. Check to see that the fractional parts in each figure add up to one.

a. The whole 6-cm-by-4-cm rectangle is worth 1.

b. The whole 8-cm-by-8-cm square is worth 1.

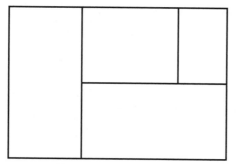
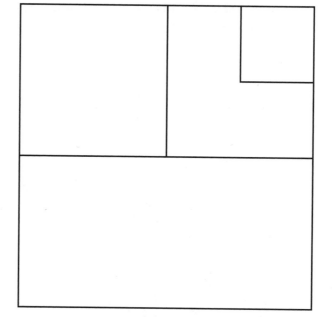

Use with Lesson 32.

Unit 4

Study Link 33: A Complicated Pizza

The pizza shown has been cut into 12 equal slices.

1. Fill in each blank with a fraction.

   _____ of the slices have **just one** type of ingredient.

   _____ of the slices have **2 or more** types of ingredients.

   _____ of the slices have **only** sausage.

   _____ of the slices have sausage as **at least one** ingredient.

   _____ of the slices have **no** vegetables.

   _____ of the slices have **both** meat and vegetables.

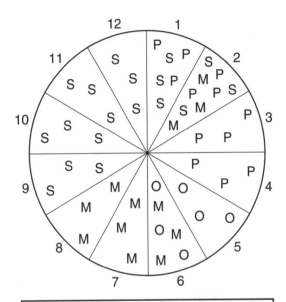

S = Sausage   P = Pepperoni
M = Mushroom   O = Onion

2. Suppose that all the slices with pepperoni are eaten first.

   How many slices remain? _____

   What fraction of the slices remaining have mushrooms? _____

   What fraction of the slices remaining have only mushrooms? _____

3. Bob, Sara, Don, and Alice share the pizza. Each person will eat exactly 3 slices.

   Bob will eat slices with only meat (sausage and pepperoni). Alice will eat slices with only vegetables (mushrooms and onions). Don hates pepperoni. Sara loves mushrooms but will eat any of the toppings.

   The slices are numbered from 1 to 12. Which slices should they take? (*Note:* There is more than one possible solution.)

   Bob: _____   Don: _____

   Sara: _____   Alice: _____

Study Link 34: Fraction-Stick Problems

1. Shade the fraction sticks to help you find equivalent fractions.

a. $\frac{1}{2} = \dfrac{\boxed{}}{8}$

b. $\frac{3}{4} = \dfrac{\boxed{}}{16}$

c. $\dfrac{\boxed{}}{4} = \frac{2}{8} = \dfrac{\boxed{}}{16}$

2. Shade the fraction sticks to help you solve the addition problems.

a. $\frac{1}{4} + \frac{3}{4} =$ _____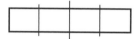

b. $\frac{1}{2} + \frac{2}{8} =$ _____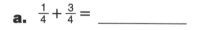

c. $\frac{1}{2} + \frac{3}{4} =$ _____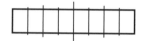

3. Shade the fraction sticks to help you solve the fraction number stories.

a. Joe was baking a cake. He added $\frac{3}{4}$ cup of white flour and $\frac{3}{8}$ cup of whole wheat flour. How much flour did he use in all?

_____cups

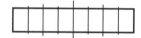

b. Twanda glued together 2 wooden boards. One board was $\frac{3}{8}$ of an inch thick. The other was $\frac{1}{2}$-inch thick. How thick is the new board?

_____inch

4. Make up a number story using fractions. Then use fraction sticks to solve it.

Number story: _____

_____

_____

Solution: _____

_____

Study Link 35: Equivalent Fractions

1. If the fractions are equivalent, write $=$ in the answer blank. If the fractions are not equivalent, write $\neq$ in the answer blank.

    a. $\frac{3}{4}$ _____ $\frac{9}{12}$ **b.** $\frac{3}{10}$ _____ $\frac{1}{5}$ **c.** $\frac{7}{14}$ _____ $\frac{8}{15}$

    d. $\frac{36}{72}$ _____ $\frac{1}{2}$ **e.** $\frac{7}{12}$ _____ $\frac{21}{36}$ **f.** $\frac{16}{100}$ _____ $\frac{8}{50}$

    g. $\frac{10}{12}$ _____ $\frac{5}{6}$ **h.** $\frac{9}{16}$ _____ $\frac{45}{48}$ **i.** $\frac{8}{3}$ _____ $\frac{16}{6}$

2. Write a fraction that is equivalent to the given fraction.

    a. $\frac{3}{5} = \frac{\Box}{10}$ **b.** $\frac{44}{55} = \frac{\Box}{5}$ **c.** $\frac{35}{60} = \frac{7}{\Box}$

    d. $\frac{2}{3} = \frac{14}{\Box}$ **e.** $\frac{12}{\Box} = \frac{3}{10}$ **f.** $\frac{\Box}{15} = \frac{6}{45}$

3. If a classroom has 28 students and $\frac{4}{7}$ are boys, how many boys are in the class? _____

4. Nikhil spent $15.00 on a CD. If that was $\frac{1}{2}$ of his monthly allowance, how much does he receive for an allowance? _____

5. Make up a number story using the fraction $\frac{3}{4}$. Then solve it.

_____

_____

_____

_____

_____

    Solution: _____

_____

Study Link 36: Decimal Numbers

1. Mark each of these numbers on the number line. The first one is done for you.

30.13   30.72   31.05   29.94   30.38

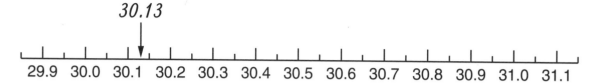

30.13

29.9 30.0 30.1 30.2 30.3 30.4 30.5 30.6 30.7 30.8 30.9 31.0 31.1

2. Below is a list of the ten smallest countries in the world. Round the area of each country to the nearest tenth of a square kilometer.

Country	Area in Square Kilometers	Area Rounded to the Nearest Tenth of a Square Kilometer
1. Vatican City	0.44 km²	km²
2. Monaco	1.89 km²	km²
3. Nauru	20.72 km²	km²
4. Tuvalu	23.96 km²	km²
5. San Marino	60.87 km²	km²
6. Liechtenstein	160.58 km²	km²
7. Marshall Islands	181.30 km²	km²
8. St. Kitts and Nevis	296.36 km²	km²
9. Maldives	297.85 km²	km²
10. Malta	315.98 km²	km²

Just a Chip Off the Old Block

In area, the United States is the fourth-largest country in the world, covering about 9,373,000 square kilometers. Rhode Island, the smallest state in the United States, covers about 4,000 square kilometers.

Source: *The Top 10 of Everything*.

How Did I Spend a Million Dollars?

Use the information from Master 26 and your Percent Circle to make a circle graph to represent your purchases. Be sure to include a title and to label each section.

Begin by drawing the section for the category that accounts for the smallest part of the $1,000,000. The category on which you spent the greatest amount of money will be marked last. Because of the rounding that you did on Master 26, your percents may not add up to exactly 100%. If so, your largest category will not be exactly correct, but it will be close enough.

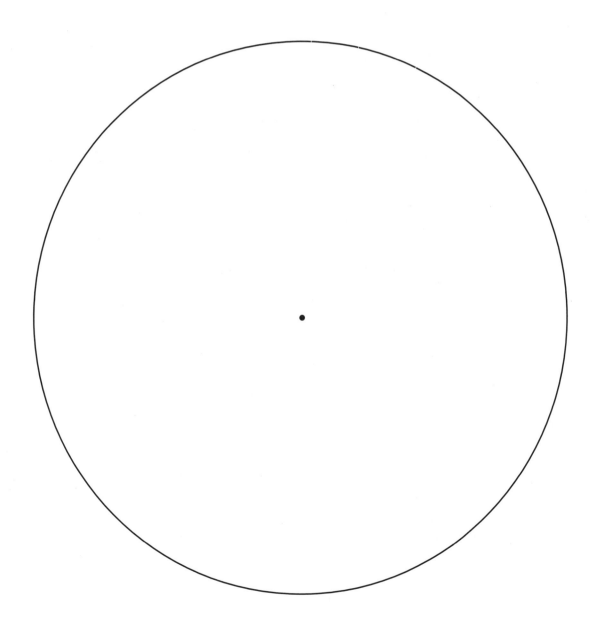

✔ Cumulative Review

1. Choose the most reasonable answer.

   a. About how long is a new pencil?   2 inches   7 inches   12 inches   1 yard

   b. About how high is the
   classroom door?   6 inches   4 feet   7 feet   1 yard

   c. About how tall is an adult?   18 inches   2 feet   2 yards   4 yards

   d. Estimate the answer to the problem 199 * 19.

       About 38,500   About 400   About 4000   About 4150

2. Use your protractor to measure the angle below.

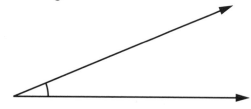

   The angle measures about _____°.

3. Of the following times, circle the ones where the minute and hour hands would form 90° angles on a standard clock-face.

   (a) 9:00   (b) 6:30

   (c) 7:25   (d) 3:00

4. Use the table to answer the questions below.

State Populations in 1900 and 1990

State	1900	1990
Massachusetts	2,805,346	6,016,425
Georgia	2,216,331	6,478,216
Michigan	2,420,982	9,295,297
Arizona	122,931	3,665,228

   a. What was the population of Massachusetts in the 1990 census? _____

   b. Which state had the largest population in 1900? _____

   c. Which state had the largest growth in number of people between 1900 and 1990? _____

   d. About how large was this increase? _____

✔ **Checking Progress** (continued)

10. The Camachos computed their budget for
an average month. They made a circle
graph showing their major expenses.

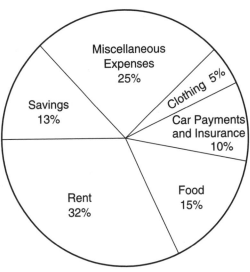

  a. What single item accounts
  for about $\frac{1}{3}$ of their
  monthly expenses?   _____

  b. Miscellaneous expenses
  make up what fraction of
  their monthly budget?   _____

  c. The Camachos spend about $1200
  per month on rent and food. About
  how much is their total monthly budget? $_____

11. This table shows the
results of a survey of
20 sixth graders. They
were asked, "What
would you do if you
had an hour free?"

Activity	Number of Students	Percent
Play a Sport	10	
Play Music	5	
Watch TV	3	
Read a Book	2	

  a. Compute the percent
  that chose each activity and fill
  in the last column in the table.

  b. Make a circle graph. Draw the
  sections and label them.

  c. Based on this information, if you
  surveyed 100 students, how many
  would you expect to choose a
  sports activity?

  _____

  Explain your answer. _____

  _____

  _____

Activities Chosen for Free Hour

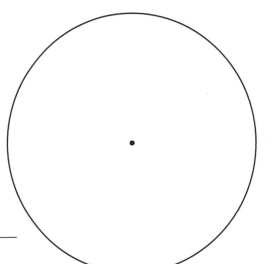

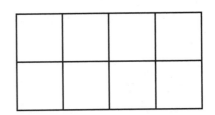

✔ Checking Progress

1. a. Shade in $\frac{2}{8}$ of the rectangle at the right.

b. $\frac{2}{8} = \dfrac{\boxed{}}{4}$

c. $\frac{2}{8} = \dfrac{\boxed{}}{16}$

2. Write the mixed number and the fraction named by each diagram below. In each diagram, the square is worth 1.

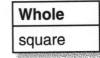

a. mixed number: _____ fraction: _____

b. mixed number: _____ fraction: _____

c. mixed number: _____ fraction: _____

d. mixed number: _____ fraction: _____

3. Use the fraction sticks to add the fractions.

a. $\frac{1}{4} + \frac{1}{4} =$ _____ = _____

b. $\frac{1}{8} + \frac{3}{8} =$ _____ = _____

c. $\frac{1}{2} + \frac{1}{4} =$ _____ = _____

d. $\frac{3}{4} + \frac{1}{2} =$ _____ = _____

4. Which amount below is closest in value to $1.50? Circle it.

5 quarters   2 half-dollars   14 dimes   15 pennies   8 quarters

5. Which of the fractions below is closest to $\frac{1}{2}$? Circle it.

$\frac{1}{3}$ $\frac{3}{2}$ $\frac{5}{8}$ $\frac{3}{4}$ $\frac{9}{10}$

Explain why you chose that fraction. _____

_____

_____

✔ **Checking Progress** (continued)

6. Match each fraction below to the equivalent decimal and/or percent.
Draw a line to connect them. Use your calculator if necessary.

a. $\frac{3}{10}$ 0.75

b. $\frac{3}{4}$ 0.3

c. $\frac{1}{4}$ 50%

d. $\frac{1}{2}$ 0.25

e. $\frac{4}{5}$ 30%

f. $\frac{30}{100}$ 0.8

7. It is estimated that about 10 out of every 100 people
are left-handed. What percent of the population is left-handed? _____

8. Of the 20 buttons Pedro picked out of a bowl,
12 were white and 8 were black.

a. What fraction were black? _____

b. What percent were black? _____

c. How many more black buttons would
Pedro need for half of the buttons to be black? _____

9. **a.** Shade in $\frac{3}{4}$ of the circle below.

b. What percent of the circle is shaded? _____

c. What percent of the circle is not shaded? _____

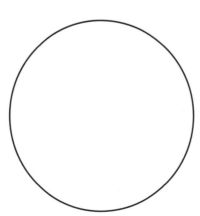

Study Link 37: Champion Tennis Players

The following table shows the number of times through 1996 that each of the following players won the four listed tennis tournaments.

Player	Australian Open	Wimbledon	French Open	U.S. Open	Total
Chris Evert Lloyd	2	3	7	6	18
Monica Seles	4	0	3	2	9
Steffi Graf	4	7	5	5	21
John McEnroe	0	3	0	4	7
Jimmy Connors	1	2	0	5	8

1. **a.** How many times did Jimmy Connors win Wimbledon? _____

   b. What is the total number of times he won the four listed tournaments? _____

   c. What fraction of this total were won at Wimbledon? _____

2. **a.** How many times did Chris Evert Lloyd win the U.S. Open? _____

   b. What is the total number of times she won the four listed tournaments? _____

   c. What fraction of this total were won at the U.S. Open? _____

   d. Write the above fraction as a decimal. _____

3. **a.** How many times has Steffi Graff won the French Open? _____

   b. What fraction is this of her total number of wins for these four tournaments? _____

   c. Write the above fraction as a decimal. Round to the nearest hundredth. _____

4. **a.** How many times has Monica Seles won the Australian Open? _____

   b. What fraction is this of her total number of wins for these four tournaments? _____

   c. Write the above fraction as a decimal. _____

Source: *The World Almanac and Book of Facts 1997.*

Study Link 38: Decimals, Fractions, or Mixed Numbers

1. The five driest inhabited places in the world and the average amount of rain they each receive each year are listed below. Convert each decimal measurement to a fraction or a mixed number.

Location	Average Annual Rainfall Expressed as a Decimal	Average Annual Rainfall Expressed as a Fraction or a Mixed Number
Aswan, Egypt	0.5 mm	$\frac{1}{2}$ mm
Luxor, Egypt	0.7 mm	mm
Arica, Chile	1.1 mm	mm
Ica, Peru	2.3 mm	mm
Antofagasta, Chile	4.9 mm	mm

2. What is the total average annual rainfall for these 5 locations?   _____ mm

3. America's longest place name is

    Chargoggagoggmanchauggagoggchaubunagungamaugg.

    This name for a lake near Webster, Massachusetts, is 45 letters long. It is a Native American name that means, "You fish on your side, I'll fish on mine, and no one fishes in the middle."

    a. What fraction of the word is made up of the letter *g*?   _____

    b. Write the above fraction as a decimal.   _____

    c. What fraction of the word is made up of the letter *c*?   _____

    d. Write the above fraction as a decimal.   _____

    e. What fraction of the word is made up of the letter *a*?   _____

    f. Write the above fraction as a decimal.   _____

Study Link 39: Emily's Vacation

Emily spent $1,000,000 on a 10-day vacation to Florida for 24 people. She was interested in finding out what percent of the money was spent on each of the different major categories. Complete the fraction, decimal, and percent conversions that she has started. Round each percent to the nearest whole-number percent.

Category	Total	Fraction	Decimal	Percent
Vacation Wardrobe	$50,750	$\frac{50,750}{1,000,000}$	0.05075	5%
Sporting Equipment	$24,100	$\frac{24,100}{1,000,000}$	0.0241	2%
Transportation	$250,640			
Lodging	$33,550			
Group Activities	$177,200			
4-Day Cruise	$154,700			
Disney Dollars	$240,000			
Free-Time and Personal Activities	$33,960			
Luggage and Camcorders	$35,030			

1. What would you expect the sum of all the percents to be? _____

2. What is the actual sum of the percents? _____

3. How can you account for this? _____

_____

_____

Study Link 40: Late-Night Snacks

One night, Mr. Lauer couldn't sleep. So he went to the kitchen, where he found a bowl full of plums. Feeling hungry, he ate $\frac{1}{6}$ of the plums.

Later that same night, Mrs. Lauer awoke hungry. She couldn't get back to sleep, so she went to the kitchen. She, too, found the plums and ate $\frac{1}{5}$ of what Mr. Lauer had left there.

Still later, the oldest daughter, Linda, awoke, went to the kitchen, and ate $\frac{1}{4}$ of the remaining plums.

Even later, her brother Tom, the oldest son, ate $\frac{1}{3}$ of what was then left.

Finally, the second daughter, Molly, ate $\frac{1}{2}$ of what was left, leaving only 4 plums for the next day's bag lunches.

How many plums were originally in the bowl? _____ plums

One way that you might try to solve this problem is to start with a pile of counters (such as beans or pennies). Be sure you start with a number of counters that is divisible by 6. Then act out the problem. Take $\frac{1}{6}$ of the counters, then take $\frac{1}{5}$ of what is left, then $\frac{1}{4}$, and so on.

Is the correct amount (4 plums) left at the end? Or is the amount left too much or too little? If you do not have 4 plums left at the end, will you try starting with a larger pile or a smaller pile? Keep trying until you finish with 4 plums.

A Costly Savings

Have you ever clipped a coupon to save money on a purchase? Coupons are not always cost efficient or good for the environment.

- Each day, businesses distribute 392 million coupons that are worth a total of over $70 million.

- This is 11 million square feet of coupons, enough to cover 250 acres.

- Sadly, less than 4% are ever redeemed.

Source: *In One Day.*

Study Link 41: Identifying Fractions and Decimal Numbers

In Problems 1–3, circle the fraction or decimal that is represented by the shaded portion in the 100-box grid.

1.

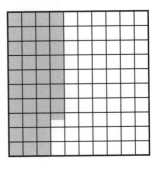

100%

(a)   0.675

(b) $\frac{3}{8}$

(c)   0.35

(d) $\frac{3}{7}$

2.

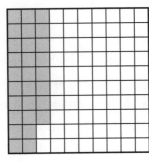

100%

(a) $\frac{2}{8}$

(b)   0.27

(c) $\frac{14}{50}$

(d)   0.29

3.

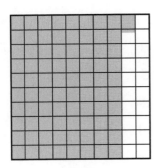

100%

(a) $\frac{5}{15}$

(b) $\frac{12}{16}$

(c) $\frac{11}{16}$

(d) $\frac{13}{16}$

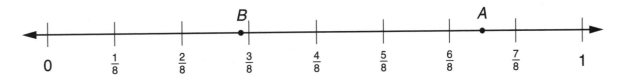

In Problems 4 and 5, use the number line above.

4. Circle the answer that corresponds to the point marked by *A*.

   (a) 0.7   (b) $\frac{11}{16}$ (c) 0.8125   (d) 0.92

5. Circle the answer that corresponds to the point marked by *B*.

   (a) $\frac{5}{16}$ (b) 0.36   (c) $\frac{1}{5}$ (d) 0.45

Up on the House Top

The roof of a house collects an average of 20,000 pounds of snow during a snowstorm.

Source: *The Average Book.*

Study Link 42: What's in a Landfill?

People who study landfills have estimated the percent of landfill space (volume) taken up by paper, food, plastic, and so on.

Space in landfills taken up by:

Paper 50%

Food & Yard waste 13%

Plastic 10%

Metal 6%

Glass 1%

Other waste 20%

> *Think of it this way:*
>
> For every 100 boxes of garbage hauled to the dump, expect that about 50 boxes could be filled with paper, 6 with metal, 1 with glass, and so on.

Source: "Once and Future Landfills," *National Geographic,* May 1991.

Cut out the Percent Circle. Use it to make a circle graph for the data in the table. (Remember to label the graph and give it a title.)

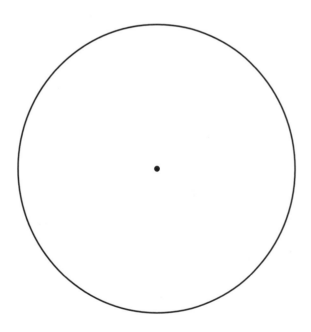

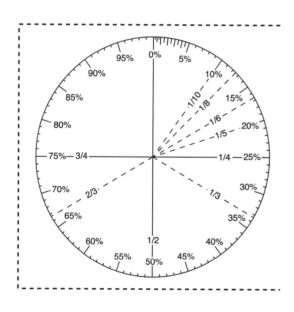

A Year of Trash

The average U.S. resident produces about 4 pounds of garbage each day. That is nearly $\frac{3}{4}$ ton of garbage each year.

Source: *1993 Information Please Environmental Almanac.*

How Will I Spend a Million Dollars?

Accounting Sheet
Totals of Major Categories

Major Category	Cost

Total   **$1,000,000**

How Will I Spend a Million Dollars?

Accounting Sheet
A Major Category—Itemized

Category: _____

Item	Quantity	Unit Price	Total Price

Total $ _____

Fraction-Stick Chart

Base-10 Grids

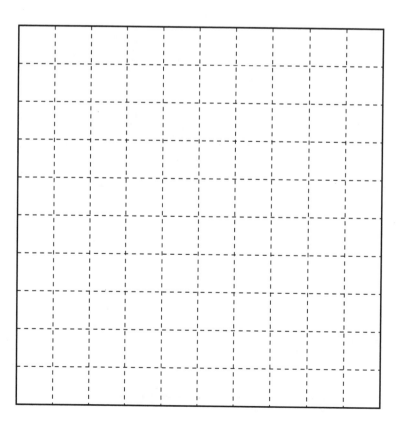

Use with Lesson 36.

Unit 4

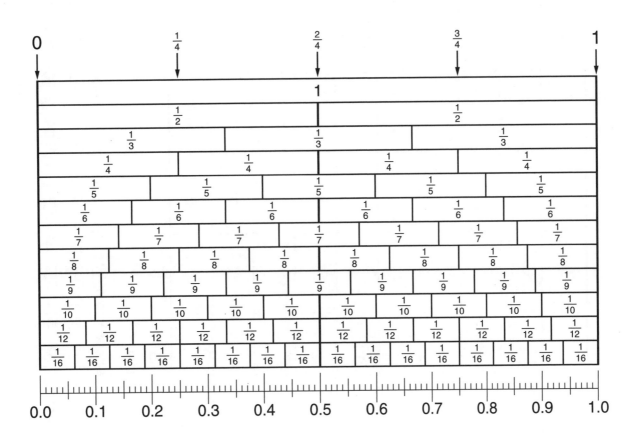

Table of Decimal Equivalents for Fractions

Example: To find the decimal equivalent for $\frac{1}{4}$, use the row for the denominator 4. Go to the column for the numerator 1. The box where the row and the column meet shows the decimal 0.25.

Denominator \ Numerator	1	2	3	4	5	6	7	8	9	10
1	1.0	2.0	3.0							
2	0.5	1.0	1.5							
3							$2.\overline{3}$			
4	0.25				1.25					
5	0.2				1.0					
6										$1.\overline{6}$
7	$0.\overline{142857}$									
8					0.625					
9								$0.\overline{8}$		
10	0.1									

Use with Lesson 38 and following.

Unit 4

Frac-Tac-Toe **Number-Card Board**

NUMERATOR PILE

PLACE CARDS FACEDOWN.

**WHEN CARDS ALL USED,
SHUFFLE AND REPLACE.**

NUMERATOR PILE

PLAY EACH CARD FACEUP.

DENOMINATOR PILE

PLACE CARDS FACEDOWN.

**WHEN CARDS ALL USED,
JUST REPLACE.
DO NOT SHUFFLE!**

DENOMINATOR PILE

PLAY EACH CARD FACEUP.

Use with Lesson 38 and following.

2-4-5-10 Frac-Tac-Toe

If you use a standard deck of playing cards:

- Use Queens as zeros (0).
- Use Aces as ones (1).
- Discard Jacks and Kings.

If you use an *Everything Math Deck,* discard cards greater than 10.

Use different color counters or coins as markers. If you use coins, one player is "heads" and the other player is "tails."

Numerator
Pile

All remaining
cards

Denominator
Pile

Two each
of 2, 4, 5,
and 10 cards

> 1.0	0 or 1	> 2.0	0 or 1	> 1.0
0.1	0.2	0.25	0.3	0.4
> 1.5	0.5	> 1.5	0.5	>1.5
0.6	0.7	0.75	0.8	0.9
> 1.0	0 or 1	> 2.0	0 or 1	> 1.0

2-4-5-10 Frac-Tac-Toe

If you use a standard deck of playing cards:

- Use Queens as zeros (0).

- Use Aces as ones (1).

- Discard Jacks and Kings.

If you use an *Everything Math Deck,*
discard cards greater than 10.

Use different color counters or coins as
markers. If you use coins, one player is
"heads" and the other player is "tails."

> **Numerator Pile**
>
> All remaining cards

> **Denominator Pile**
>
> Two each of 2, 4, 5, and 10 cards

>100%	0% or 100%	>200%	0% or 100%	>100%
10%	20%	25%	30%	40%
>100%	50%	>200%	50%	>100%
60%	70%	75%	80%	90%
>100%	0% or 100%	>200%	0% or 100%	>100%

Percent Circle

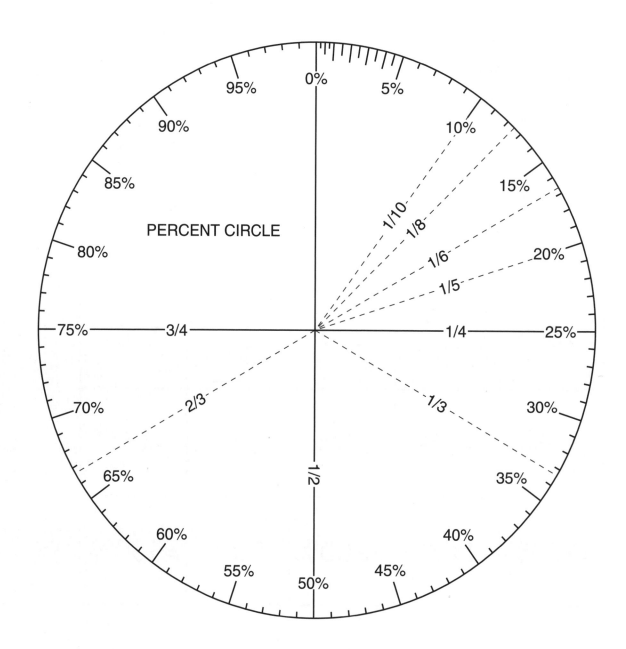

2-4-5-10 *Frac-Tac-Toe* (Bingo Version)

If you use a standard deck of playing cards:

- Use Queens as zeros (0).
- Use Aces as ones (1).
- Discard Jacks and Kings.

If you use an *Everything Math Deck,*
discard cards greater than 10.

Fill in each gameboard by entering these
numbers in the empty spaces.

0	0	0.1	0.2
0.25	0.3	0.4	0.5
0.5	0.6	0.7	0.75
0.8	0.9	1	1

Numerator
Pile

All remaining
cards

Denominator
Pile

Two each
of 2, 4, 5,
and 10 cards

> 1.0		> 2.0		> 1.0
> 1.5		> 1.5		>1.5
> 1.0		> 2.0		> 1.0

2-4-5-10 Frac-Tac-Toe (Bingo Version)

If you use a standard deck of playing cards:

- Use Queens as zeros (0).

- Use Aces as ones (1).

- Discard Jacks and Kings.

If you use an *Everything Math Deck,* discard cards greater than 10.

Fill in each gameboard by entering these numbers in the empty spaces.

0%	0%	10%	20%
25%	30%	40%	50%
50%	60%	70%	75%
80%	90%	100%	100%

Numerator Pile

All remaining cards

Denominator Pile

Two each of 2, 4, 5, and 10 cards

>100%		>200%		>100%
>100%		>200%		>100%
>100%		>200%		>100%

Project: How Would You Spend a Million Dollars?

MASTER 25

1. What was the most difficult part of creating your million-dollar project? Explain.

_____

_____

_____

_____

_____

2. What was the best part of your project? Explain.

_____

_____

_____

_____

_____

3. What new mathematical knowledge did you gain by doing this project? Explain.

_____

_____

_____

_____

_____

4. What did you learn about yourself by completing this project?

_____

_____

_____

_____

_____

Million-Dollar Categories

Use your accounting sheets to list all of the major categories from the How Would You Spend a Million Dollars? project in the spaces provided below. Calculate the fractions, decimals, and percents. Round each percent to the nearest whole number.

Category	Total $ Spent	Fraction	Decimal	Percent
		____ / 1,000,000		
		____ / 1,000,000		
		____ / 1,000,000		
		____ / 1,000,000		
		____ / 1,000,000		
		____ / 1,000,000		
		____ / 1,000,000		
		____ / 1,000,000		
		____ / 1,000,000		
		____ / 1,000,000		
		____ / 1,000,000		
		____ / 1,000,000		
		____ / 1,000,000		

Unit 5

Collecting & Working with Data

Study Link: Parent Letter

Unit 5: Collecting and Working with Data

The authors of *Everyday Mathematics* believe that students should do serious and substantial work with data. Unit 5 provides many activities designed to present and teach relevant data skills and concepts, allowing your child ample opportunities to practice organizing and analyzing the data he or she collects.

The data that your child initially collects will usually consist of an unorganized collection of numbers. Several devices, such as number-line plots, picture groupings, tally charts, and bar graphs made from self-stick notes are used throughout the lessons in Unit 5 to help your child organize data.

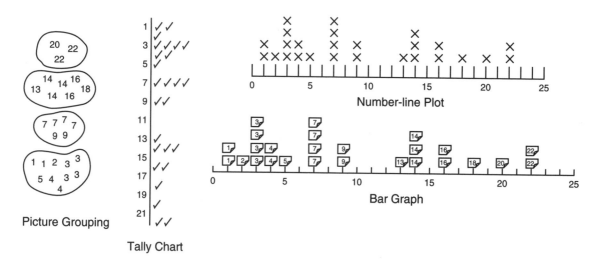

Picture Grouping

Tally Chart

Number-line Plot

Bar Graph

After organizing the data using a variety of methods, your child will study the **landmarks** of the data. The following terms are called landmarks because they show the important features of the data:

- The **maximum** is the largest data value observed.
- The **minimum** is the smallest data value observed.
- The **range** is the difference between the maximum and the minimum.
- The **mode** is the "most popular" data value or the value observed most often.
- The **median** is the middle data value observed.

At the end of the unit students will have an opportunity to demonstrate their skills in this area by conducting a survey of their peers, gathering and organizing the data, analyzing their results, and writing a summary report.

Finally, your child will continue his or her work with the American Tour by studying a variety of Native American measurements for length and distance based on parts of the body. Students will convert these body measures to personal measures by measuring their fingers, hands, and arms in both metric and U.S. customary units. In addition, your child will learn how to read a variety of contour-type maps, such as climate, precipitation, and growing-seasons maps.

Study Link 47: Comparing Left and Right Hands

Which is more flexible—the hand you write with or your other hand?
This activity will help you find out.

Read the instructions below. Then, on the back of this paper, trace and
measure your right and left hands.

Trace Your Hands

1. In the air, stretch to make the largest possible angle between the thumb
   and little finger on one of your hands.

2. Now, lay that hand down on the paper and use your other hand to trace
   around that hand with a pen or pencil. Label the tracing "right" or "left."

3. Repeat Steps 1 and 2 for your other hand.

Mark and Measure

1. On each tracing, draw straight lines through the middle of the little finger
   and thumb outlines. Be sure the lines intersect, forming an angle. (See the
   picture below.)

2. Use your circular protractor to measure the angle formed by each hand.
   Record your answers below.

   Angle formed by right thumb and little finger: _____

   Angle formed by left thumb and little finger: _____

   I write with my _____ hand.
                    (right or left?)

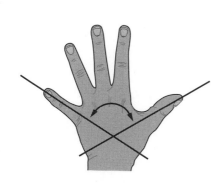

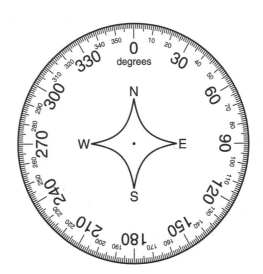

Study Link 48: How Much Do Students Spend?

How much do students spend for books, CDs, and other items? One magazine surveyed 750 students, ages 9 to 14, to find out. Here are some of the results:

- A median amount of $5 per week was spent for books and magazines.

- A median amount of $10 per week was spent for tapes and CDs.

- A median amount of $4 per week was spent for movie tickets.

The number-line plots below represent data from the survey. One plot shows weekly spending for books and magazines. One plot shows spending for tapes and CDs. One shows spending for movie tickets.

Match the plots with the items. Which plot is for books and magazines? Which is for tapes and CDs? Which is for movie tickets?

Write in the correct title for each number-line plot. Each X represents 50 students.

Spending for _____ **in 1 Week**

```
          X   X
          X   X
      X   X   X           X
      X   X   X   X   X       X           X
 ───────────────────────────────────────────────────────
  0   1   2   3   4   5   6   7   8   9  10  11  12  13  14  15  16  17  18
```

Spending for _____ **in 1 Week**

```
                      X
      X   X   X       X
  X   X   X   X   X   X   X           X               X                   X
 ───────────────────────────────────────────────────────
  0   1   2   3   4   5   6   7   8   9  10  11  12  13  14  15  16  17  18
```

Spending for _____ **in 1 Week**

```
                                      X
              X               X       X
      X   X   X   X   X       X   X   X   X           X       X
 ───────────────────────────────────────────────────────
  0   1   2   3   4   5   6   7   8   9  10  11  12  13  14  15  16  17  18
```

Study Link 52: How Do People Fold Their Hands?

Ask at least three friends or family members to fold their hands. Do not give a reason.

Observe which thumb is on top. Record the results below.

Circle "Right" or "Left."

Person #1:   Right   Left

Person #2:   Right   Left

Person #3:   Right   Left

Person #4:   Right   Left

Person #5:   Right   Left

A Big Hand

Serge Rachmaninoff was a famous 20th-century Russian composer and pianist. His hands were unusually large. He could span a "twelfth" at the piano keyboard. (If you press down a white piano key with your thumb, and another white key with your little finger, and there are 10 other white keys in between, you are playing a twelfth.)

This means that Rachmaninoff's great span was about 28 centimeters.

Circles

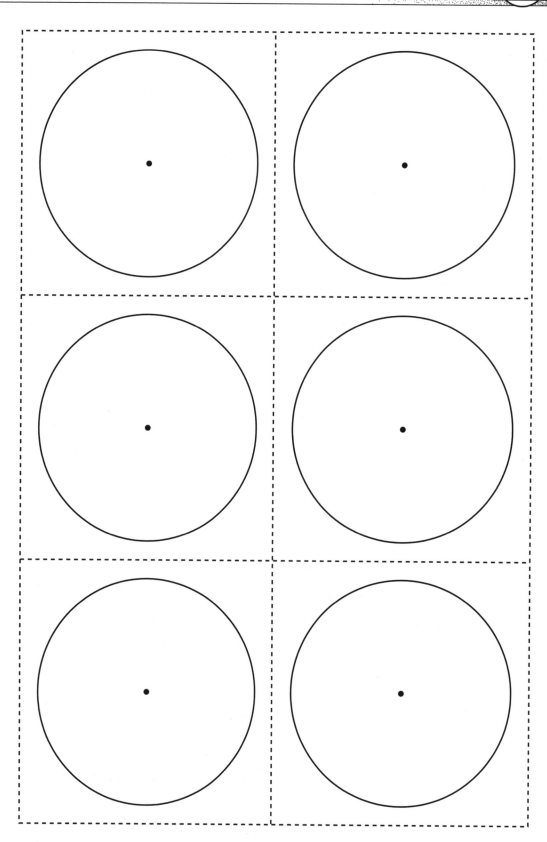

Survey Project: Suggested Questions

Change the questions if necessary. For example, maybe no one takes a train to your school. Read the questions aloud. Each student being interviewed should write his or her answers on a sheet of paper.

1. How did you travel to school this morning?

   Did you walk?

   Did you ride a bicycle?

   Did you ride in a car?

   Did you take a school bus? A city bus?

   Did you take a train? A subway?

   Or did you travel some other way?

   Write your answer on your paper.

2. How many minutes did it take you to get to school—from the time you left home until you got to school?

   You may not remember the exact time. Just make your best estimate.

   Write your answer on your paper.

3. Think about when school starts in the morning and ends in the afternoon.

   I'll read five statements. Write the letter of the one you most agree with:

   a. School should start 30 minutes earlier and end 30 minutes earlier.

   b. School should start 15 minutes earlier and end 15 minutes earlier.

   c. School starts and ends at about the right time.

   d. School should start 15 minutes later and end 15 minutes later.

   e. School should start 30 minutes later and end 30 minutes later.

Read the 5 choices again.

Thank everyone, and collect the papers.

Survey Project: Classroom Summary Sheet

Teacher's Name: _____ Grade _____

Interviewers: _____

Question:	Tally

Question:	Tally

In a stem-and-leaf plot, record the responses for the question that was answered using a measure. Do the plot on the back of this paper.

Stems (10s)	Leaves (1s)

Question: _____

_____

_____

_____

✔ Checking Progress

6. Eleven babies were born at Central Community Hospital. Their lengths in millimeters are given below:

516 527 510 507 520 495 503 485 518 525 510

a. Give the following landmarks for this data:

median: _____ maximum: _____ minimum: _____

NO

b. Circle the stem-and-leaf plot below that shows this data.

Stems (100s and 10s)	Leaves (1s)	Stems (100s and 10s)	Leaves (1s)	Stems (100s and 10s)	Leaves (1s)
48	5 5	48	5	48	5
49	3	49	5	49	5
50	0 7	50	3 7	50	0 3 7
51	0 0 6 8 9	51	0 0 6 8	51	8 9 9
52	5	52	0 5 7	52	0 0 5

7. Make up a set of data with the following landmarks. There should be at least 7 numbers in your set.

The median is 12.   The maximum is 15.

The minimum is 1.   The mode is 10.

_____

_____

_____

_____

_____

_____

Unit 6

Division, Ratios, & Exponential Notation

Study Link: Parent Letter

Unit 6: Division, Ratios, and Exponential Notation

In *Fourth Grade Everyday Mathematics,* students were introduced to a nonstandard division algorithm. This algorithm was emphasized because it is easy to learn, builds upon a student's multiplication and number knowledge, and can be quickly employed by students who struggle with traditional computation. Equipped with this algorithm or a calculator, every student should be able to solve even the most complicated division problems.

After your child has worked with this division algorithm, you might ask him or her to explain the example below:

$7\overline{)127}$	10	Write an estimate.
70		Write 10 * 7.
57	5	Subtract. Estimate again.
35		Write 5 * 7.
22	3	Subtract. Estimate again.
21		Write 3 * 7.
1		Subtract.
	18	Total the estimates.

In this unit, your child will have many opportunities to practice using this division algorithm, as well as others of his or her choosing. Special attention will be placed on interpreting the remainder of a division problem. Challenge your child to a game of *Division Dash* to assist in practicing this algorithm.

The American Tour continues as the class explores a political map of the United States and the electoral college. Students play *Arithmetic Election* to review of variety of skills. Your child will also refer to the *American Tour Almanac* as part of a discussion on ratios.

Students will also work with exponential notation and will be introduced to scientific notation. If you enjoy the game *Division Dash* at the beginning of the unit, you might want to play *Exponent Ball* with your child during these lessons.

Other topics will include the use of parentheses to punctuate mathematical expressions so they are unambiguous, and applications of negative numbers. Your child will play a new version of *Frac-Tac-Toe* to practice fraction, decimal, and percent conversions.

Study Link 53: Estimating the Number of Cats

> There are about 250 million people and
> 100 million households in the United States.

Estimation Plan: What information do you need in order to estimate the number of cats in the United States? Where will you try to find this information?

_____

_____

_____

_____

_____

_____

I estimate that there are about _____ cats in the United States.

Explain how you made your estimate.

_____

_____

_____

_____

_____

_____

_____

_____

Study Link 54: Using Fact Knowledge

1. Complete the following division problems. Look for patterns.

    a.   24 / 8 = _____   **b.**   240 / 8 = _____
    Think: How many 8s in 24?   *Think:* How many 8s in 240?

    c.   240 / 80 = _____   **d.** 2400 / 80 = _____
    Think: How many 80s in 240?   *Think:* How many 80s in 2400?

    e. 2400 / 800 = _____   **f.**   2400 / 8 = _____

    g.   35 / 7 = _____   **h.**   350 / 7 = _____

    i.   360 / 6 = _____   **j.** 3600 / 60 = _____

    k. 5000 / 500 = _____   **l.**   5000 / 5 = _____

2. You can use your fact knowledge by breaking the dividend into parts that are easy to divide. For example, to divide 96 by 3 mentally, you can break 96 into two or more numbers that are easy to divide by 3.

    96 / 3 = ?
      Think: 96 = 90 + 6
    How many 3s in 90?
      30 because 3 * 30 = 90
    How many 3s in 6?
      2 because 3 * 2 = 6
    Find the total number of 3s.
      30 + 2 = 32
    So, 96 divided by 3 equals 32.
    Check the result.
      3 * 32 = 96

    Use this strategy to complete the following:

    a. 72 / 3 = _____   **b.**   84 / 6 = _____

    c. 65 / 5 = _____   **d.** 120 / 5 = _____

Study Link 57: Everything You Do... More or Less

Part A

Put a check mark in the boxes next to all the sports that you participated in more than once during the past year.

❑ Basketball   ❑ Bowling   ❑ Soccer   ❑ Tennis   ❑ Volleyball

Part B

Write a story about what your life might be like if suddenly

- everything became 10 times larger or 10 times more,

    OR

- everything became 10 times smaller or 10 times less.

Use your imagination, but be specific. Give counts and measurements. Compare the way things are now with the way they would become.

Example: If everything were 10 times less, I could get to school in 2 minutes instead of the 20 minutes it takes me now. There would be only 3 people on the bus instead of the usual 30. And my lunch would cost 10 cents instead of $1.00.

_____

_____

_____

_____

_____

_____

_____

_____

_____

_____

Study Link 58: Exponents

1. In exponential notation, the exponent tells how many times the base is a factor.

   For example, $4^3 = 4 * 4 * 4 = 64$

   Each of the problems below has a mistake. Find the mistake and tell what it is. Then solve the problem.

   a. $5^2 = 5 * 2 = 10$

   Mistake: _____

   _____

   _____

   _____

   Correct solution: _____

   b. $6^3 = 3 * 3 * 3 * 3 * 3 * 3 = 729$

   Mistake: _____

   _____

   _____

   _____

   Correct solution: _____

   c. $10^4 = 10 + 10 + 10 + 10 = 40$

   Mistake: _____

   _____

   _____

   _____

   Correct solution: _____

   d. $5^4 = 5 * 4 * 5 * 4 * 5 = 2000$

   Mistake: _____

   _____

   _____

   _____

   Correct solution: _____

2. Which is bigger? Use the > (is greater than), < (is less than), or = (is equal to) symbol.

   a. 10^2 _____ 2^{10}

   b. 3^4 _____ 9^2

   c. 1^2 _____ 1^5

   d. 5^4 _____ 500

Study Link 61: Guides for Powers of 10

There are prefixes that name powers of 10. You know some of them from the metric system—for example, *kilo-* in "kilometer" (1000 meters). It's helpful to memorize the prefixes for every third power of 10 through one trillion.

$$10^3 = 10 * 10 * 10 = 1000$$

exponent — base — factors — product

Memorize the table at the right. Have a friend quiz you. Then cover the table and try to complete the statements below.

Number	Exponential Notation	Prefix
one thousand	10^3	kilo-
one million	10^6	mega-
one billion	10^9	giga-
one trillion	10^{12}	tera-

1. More than 10^9 or one _____ people live in China.

2. One thousand or $10^{\square}$ feet is a little less than $\frac{1}{5}$ of a mile.

3. Astronomers estimate that there are more than 10^{12} or

   one _____ stars in the universe.

4. More than one million or $10^{\square}$ copies of *The New York Times* are sold every day.

5. A kiloton equals one _____ or $10^{\square}$ metric tons.

6. A megaton equals one _____ or $10^{\square}$ metric tons.

Challenge

7. How far back in time would you travel if you went back 10^3 minutes? If you went back 10^6 minutes? 10^9 minutes? 10^{12} minutes? (Remember that a million is 1000 thousands; a billion is 1000 millions; and a trillion is 1000 billions.)

   _____

   _____

   _____

Study Link 62: Interpreting Scientific Notation

Scientific notation is a short way to represent large and small numbers.

In scientific notation, a number is written as the product of two factors. One factor is a whole number or decimal. The other factor is a power of 10.

Scientific notation: $4 * 10^4$

Meaning: Multiply 10^4 (10,000) by 4.
$$4 * 10^4 = 4 * 10,000 = 40,000$$

Guides for Powers of 10	
10^3	one thousand
10^6	one million
10^9	one billion
10^{12}	one trillion

Scientific notation: $6 * 10^6$

Meaning: Multiply 10^6 (1,000,000) by 6.
$$6 * 10^6 = 6 * 1,000,000 = 6,000,000$$

Complete the following statements:

1. The area of Alaska is about $6 * 10^5$ or _____ thousand square miles. The area of the "lower 48" states is about $3 * 10^6$ or

   _____ million square miles.

2. There are about $5 * 10^9$ or _____ billion people in the world.

3. It is estimated that about $5 * 10^8$ or _____ people speak English as their first or second language.

4. The language spoken by the greatest number of people is Chinese.

   More than $1 * 10^9$ or _____ people speak Chinese.

5. It is estimated that the most popular television shows in the United States are watched by at least one person in each of $4 * 10^7$ or

   _____ households.

Source: *The Universal Almanac.*

2-4-8 Frac-Tac-Toe (Bingo Version)

If you use a standard deck of playing cards:

- Use Queens as zeros (0).
- Use Aces as ones (1).
- Discard Jacks and Kings.

If you use an *Everything Math Deck,*
discard cards greater than 10.

Fill in each gameboard by entering these
numbers in the empty spaces.

0	0	0.125	0.25
0.375	0.5	0.5	0.625
0.75	0.875	1	1
1.5	1.5	2	2

Numerator Pile

All remaining cards

Denominator Pile

Two each
of 2, 4,
and 8 cards

> 2.0		> 1.5		> 2.0
> 1.0		0.25 or 0.75		>1.0
> 2.0		1.125		> 2.0

2-4-8 Frac-Tac-Toe (Bingo Version)

If you use a standard deck of playing cards:

- Use Queens as zeros (0).
- Use Aces as ones (1).
- Discard Jacks and Kings.

If you use an *Everything Math Deck,* discard cards greater than 10.

Fill in each gameboard by entering these numbers in the empty spaces.

0%	0%	$12\frac{1}{2}$%	25%
$37\frac{1}{2}$%	50%	50%	$62\frac{1}{2}$%
75%	$87\frac{1}{2}$%	100%	100%
150%	150%	200%	200%

Numerator
Pile

All remaining
cards

Denominator
Pile

Two each
of 2, 4,
and 8 cards

>200%		>150%		>200%
>100%		25 % or 75 %		>100%
>200%		$112\frac{1}{2}$%		>200%

✔ Cumulative Review

1. Fifteen fifth graders were asked how many blocks they lived from school. The following graph shows their results:

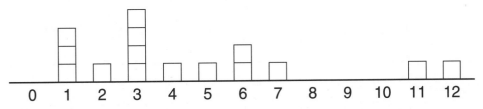

0   1   2   3   4   5   6   7   8   9   10   11   12

a. What is the maximum number of blocks from school? _____

b. What is the minimum number of blocks? _____

c. What is the range? _____

d. What is the mode? _____

e. What is the median? _____

2. Which of the following figures have an even number of right angles?

M   N   O   P

(Circle one answer below)

(a) All of them.   (b) M, N, and O, but not P.

(c) M and O, but not N or P.   (d) Only M.

3. I am a polygon.
None of my angles is greater than 90 degrees.
No two of my sides are parallel.

a. Which figure in Problem 2 fits this description? _____

b. What type of figure is polygon P in Problem 2? _____

Ladder Method

✔ **1.** **a.** 54 / 6 = _____   **b.**   9 * _____ = 630

   c. 9)‾135‾   **d.** 20)‾310‾   **e.** 12)‾255‾   **f.** 25)‾231‾

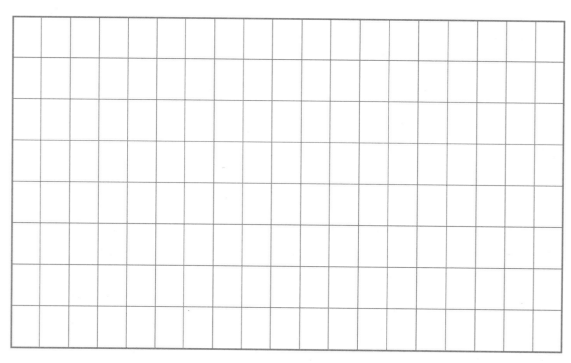

2. Tammy and her father made 130 ounces of
apple sauce. How many 8-ounce jars can they fill?   _____

Challenge

3. The go-carts cost $3 per ride. Jim has $14.
How many times can he ride a go-cart?   _____

Challenge

4. For relay races, the gym teacher divided the
class into 4 teams with an equal number of
students on each team. There were 30 students
in the class. Extra students sat out the race.

   a. How many members were on each team?   _____

   b. How many students were left over?   _____

   c. How could the class be divided into teams so that no one is left out?

   _____

   _____

   _____

✔ Checking Progress

MASTER
44

5. After collecting eggs, Farmer O'Brien puts them in boxes of a dozen each.

   a. If he collects 52 eggs, how many boxes can he fill? _____

   b. How many eggs are left? _____

   c. Is this more or less than one-half of another box? _____

6. **a.** 75 / 15 = _____

   b. Make up a division number story to go with this problem.

   _____

   _____

   _____

   _____

7. The number sentences below are not true as they are written. Insert parentheses to make each one true.

   a. $3 + 4 * 3 = 21$

   b. $16 - 8 / 2 = 4$

   c. $12 + 12 + 12 = 3 * 6 + 6$

   d. $3 * 4 + 8 - 20 = 4 * 4$

8. Write the following in <u>standard</u> notation:

   a. $7^2 = 7 * 7 =$ _____   **b.** $2^4 =$ _____

   c. $10^5 =$ _____   **d.** $5^3 =$ _____

   Write the following in <u>exponential notation</u>:

   e. $6 * 6 * 6 * 6 =$ _____

9. Draw lines to match the numbers in exponential notation with their word names.

    a. 10^{12} one thousand

    b. 10^{6} one trillion

    c. 10^{5} one hundred thousand

    d. 10^{3} one million

10. Use the information in the table to answer the questions below.

Year	U.S. Population	Number of Children Ages 5 to 14
1900	76,000,000	17,000,000
1990	255,000,000	28,000,000

    a. In 1900, what fraction of the population was from 5 to 14 years old? (Circle one.)

         About $\frac{1}{7}$ About $\frac{1}{4}$ About $\frac{1}{2}$ About $\frac{3}{4}$

    b. In 1990, what was the ratio for the following?

$$\frac{\text{Number of Children Ages 5 to 14}}{\text{Total U.S. Population}}$$

    (Circle one.)

         About $\frac{1}{10}$ About $\frac{1}{4}$ About $\frac{1}{2}$ About $\frac{1}{28}$

    c. Between 1900 and 1990, what happened to the population of the United States? (Circle one.)

         About doubled.   About tripled.   Decreased.   Stayed about the same.

11. Some scientists estimate the universe to be around eight billion years old.

    a. Write eight billion in standard notation: _____

    b. Write eight billion in scientific notation: _____

✔ Checking Progress

Review for Units 1–6

1. Draw two different arrays, each with 16 dots.

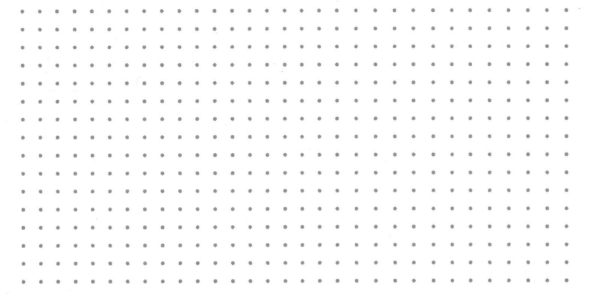

2. Circle all the numbers below that are factors of 48.

   2   4   5   6   12   14   20   24

3. Find the missing angle measurements below. (You don't need your protractor.)

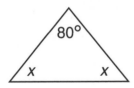

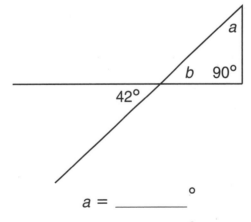

The two angles marked *x*
have the same measurement.

x = _____ °

a = _____ °

b = _____ °

✓ Checking Progress (continued)

MASTER
47

4. **a.** 24 * 9 = _____ **b.** 30 * 25 = _____ **c.** 211 * 46 = _____

   d. 205 − 148 = _____ **e.** 8.05 − 1.55 = _____ **f.** 140 / 20 = _____

5. Jenna earns $12 per day pet-sitting for her
   neighbor's dog. If she pet-sits for 8 days,
   how much will she earn? _____

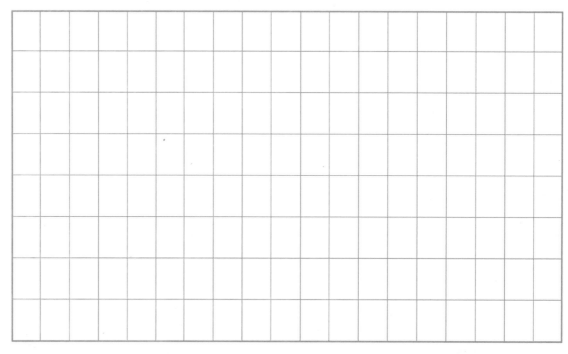

6. Evelyn timed how long it took her to travel to work on nine different days.
   Following are the times in minutes:

   45   42   45   55   48   50   35   58   44

   a. What was the   **b.** What was the
        median time? _____   maximum time? _____

   c. What was the   **d.** What was the
        minimum time? _____   range of times? _____

   e. If you were Evelyn, how much time would you
        allow to travel to work, based on these data? _____

        Explain your reasoning. _____

        _____

7. A figure is partly hidden. Which of the following might it be?
(Circle all the possible answers.)

rectangle   triangle   trapezoid   square

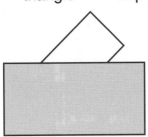

8. Add. Use the fraction sticks to help.

a. $\frac{1}{2} + \frac{1}{4} =$ _____

b. $\frac{3}{8} + \frac{1}{4} =$ _____

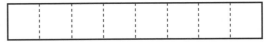

c. $\frac{3}{4} + \frac{3}{4} =$ _____

d. $\frac{1}{8} + \frac{1}{2} =$ _____

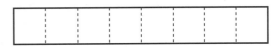

9. Circle the numbers below that are greater than $\frac{1}{2}$.

$\frac{1}{4}$ $\frac{9}{10}$ 0.66 $\frac{5}{20}$ $\frac{4}{8}$ 0.09

10. **a.** Shade approximately $\frac{3}{4}$ of the interior of the circle.

b. What percent of the interior is shaded? _____

c. Which of the fractions below does the shaded part
represent? (Circle all the possible answers.)

$\frac{6}{8}$ $\frac{3}{8}$ $\frac{5}{6}$ $\frac{75}{100}$

✓ Checking Progress (continued)

11. Simeon was writing a report on trees
in his town. He counted the different
types of trees in his neighborhood and
made a circle graph. Use his circle
graph to answer these questions:

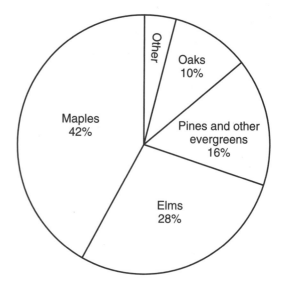

   a. What was the most
   common type of tree? _____

   b. Which types of trees
   made up one-fourth or
   more of the sample? _____

   _____

   c. If there were a total of
   100 trees in his sample, how many would be oaks? _____

   d. If there were a total
   of 50 trees, how many would be elms? _____

   e. What percent of the trees were "Other" types? _____

   f. Simeon concluded that maples are the most
   common type of tree in the United States. Do you agree? _____

   Explain your answer. _____

   _____

   _____

12. Tim plans to take the train from Boston to Smallville. The train takes 45
minutes to get from Boston to Middleton. After a wait in Middleton, the train
takes 38 minutes to get to Smallville. Tim wonders how long it will take to
travel from Boston to Smallville. What additional information does he need?

_____

_____

13. On the back of this page, draw a rectangle that has a base 4 cm long and
a height of 6.5 cm. Use your ruler or any other tool that you wish.

Unit 7

Coordinates, Area, & Circles

Study Link: Parent Letter

Unit 7: Coordinates, Area, and Circles

The beginning of this unit will provide your child with practice in locating ordered number pairs on a coordinate grid. Negative numbers, fractions, and whole numbers will be used as coordinates. Your child will play a new game, *Hidden Treasure* (similar to the commercially available game *Battleship*), which provides additional practice with coordinates. You may wish to challenge your child to a round.

In previous grades, your child studied the **perimeters** (distances around) and the areas (amounts of surface) of geometric figures. *Fourth Grade Everyday Mathematics* developed and applied formulas for the areas of rectangles, parallelograms, and triangles. In this unit, your child will review these formulas and explore new area topics, including the rectangle method for finding area, Pick's Formula for finding the area of a figure on a square grid, and the area of a circle.

Students will also examine how area, perimeter, and angle measurements are affected when a figure is enlarged or reduced. A copier-machine metaphor is used in these lessons. If you have access to a copier, it will be helpful to show your child how a document can be enlarged or reduced.

The American Tour project will continue, with students learning how public lands were surveyed and divided. In this context, the acre is described and defined. Additionally, students are given the dimensions of the playing surfaces for a variety of sports. They calculate the area of each playing surface and identify those larger than 1 acre. You and your child may wish to estimate in square feet the area of your yard, a nearby park or playground, or a parking lot or shopping mall—and then use a calculator to convert this area to acres (1 acre = 43,560 square feet).

Study Link 66: Matching Graphs to Number Stories

1. Draw a line matching each graph below to the number story that it best fits.

   a. Juanita started with $350. She saved another $25 every week.

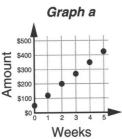

   Graph a

   b. Meredith received $350 for her birthday. She deposited the entire amount in the bank. Every week she withdrew $50.

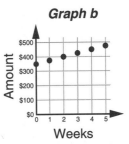

   Graph b

   c. Julian started a new savings account with $50. Every week after that he deposited $75.

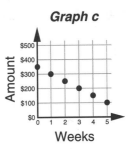

   Graph c

2. Explain how you decided which graph matches which number story.

   _____

   _____

   _____

   _____

   _____

3. Circle the rule below that best fits the number story in Problem 1a above.

   a. Savings = $350 + (25 * number of weeks)

   b. Savings = $350 − (25 * number of weeks)

   c. Savings = $350 * number of weeks

Study Link 67: The Most Common Words

The 32 most commonly used words in the English language are:

a, all, and, are, as, at, be, but, for, had, have, he, him, his, I, in,
is, it, not, of, on, one, said, so, that, the, they, to, was, we, with, you.

1. Look in a book, newspaper, or magazine and pick a writing sample that is *exactly* 25 words long. One way is to start at the beginning of a paragraph and count 25 words. Record the source of your sample.

_____

2. Make a tally mark for every word in your sample that is on the list above. Some words may occur more than once. Be sure to make a tally mark every time the word occurs. Record the total number of times any of the 32 most common words occur in your sample.

_____

The Longest Words

The longest word to be published in a dictionary first appeared in the 1982 supplement to the *Oxford English Dictionary:*

Pneumonoultramicroscopicsilicovolcanoconiosis

It has 45 letters and is defined as "a factitious [made-up] word alleged to mean 'a lung disease caused by the inhalation of very fine silica dust,' but occurring chiefly as an instance of a very long word."

In New Zealand, there is a place whose name is even longer. It has 57 letters:

Taumatawhakatangihangakoauauotamateapokaiwhenvakitanatahu

Source: *The Oxford Guide to Word Games.*

© 1999 Everyday Learning Corporation

Study Link 67: The Most Common Words (continued)

The diagram at the right represents the 20,000 most commonly used words in the English language. The area of each box in the diagram represents the number of times the words in the box occur, compared to the total.

① a and he I in is it of that the to was

② all are as at be but for had have him his not on one said so they we with you

③ about an back been before big by call came can come could did do down each first from get go has her here if into just like little look made make me more much must my no new now off only or our over other out right see she some their them then there this two up want well went who were what when where which will your

④ This space represents 19,900 other words. There is not enough room to show these words.

3. How many words are in each box?

Box 1: _____   Box 2: _____

Box 3: _____   Box 4: _____

4. About what is the area of each box?

Box 1: _____ cm²   Box 2: _____ cm²

Box 3: _____ cm²   Box 4: _____ cm²

5. What is the total area of the diagram?   about _____ cm²

6. What fraction of the total area of the diagram is each box?

Box 1: _____   Box 2: _____   Box 3: _____   Box 4: _____

Study Link 68: A Piece of Each State

A recent novelty gift offered U.S. citizens the opportunity to own land in each of the 50 states for only $49.95. However, there was a trick. The offer was for a mere *1 square inch* of land in each state.

1. About how much would it cost per square inch for a
   U.S. citizen to accept this offer?   _____

2. What fraction of 1 square yard is 50 square inches?   _____

In China, prices for 50 square inches of land in the United States were much higher. In Guangzhou, the price was about $468, in Beijing $700, and in Shanghai $1,700. When buying this land, many Chinese citizens believed that they would be able to obtain a visa to visit the United States to inspect their property. Unfortunately, this was not true.

3. About how much would it cost per square inch for a Chinese citizen to accept this offer in:

   Guangzhou?   _____

   Beijing?   _____

   Shanghai?   _____

4. About how much would it cost a Chinese citizen to buy a total of
   1 square yard of land in the United States if purchased in:

   Guangzhou?   _____

   Beijing?   _____

   Shanghai?   _____

Challenge

How many pieces of land, 1 square inch in area, are there in 1 acre?

_____

Source: *New York Times.*

Study Link 69: Calculating Area

1. Determine the area of the shaded path on the grid below.

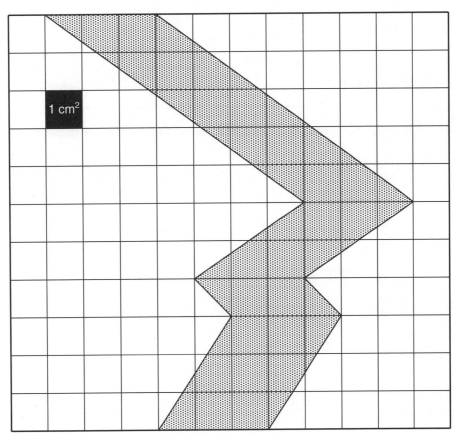

The area of the path is about _____ cm².

2. Describe the strategy that you used to calculate the area of the path.

_____

_____

_____

_____

Study Link 70: Areas of Geometric Figures

Area Formulas
Rectangle: $A = b * h$
Parallelogram: $A = b * h$
Triangle: $A = \frac{1}{2} * b * h$
A is the area, b is the length of the base, and h is the height.

---

1. Calculate the area of each figure. Pay close attention to the units.

a. The area of triangle *PIT* is

_____.
                    Unit

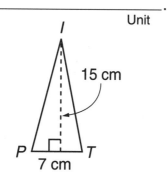

b. The area of rectangle *TOAD* is

_____.
                    Unit

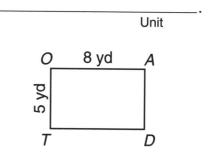

c. The area of square *BLUE* is

_____.
                    Unit

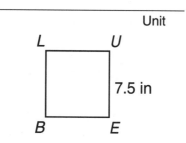

d. The area of parallelogram *COAT* is

_____.
                    Unit

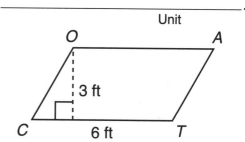

2. The area of a rectangle is 50 square feet. What are some of the possible dimensions of the rectangle?

a. Length of base = _____   Height = _____

b. Length of base = _____   Height = _____

c. Length of base = _____   Height = _____

Study Link 71: Area and Perimeter of Polygons

Find the perimeter and area of each polygon.

1. Perimeter: _____ units

Area: _____ units^2

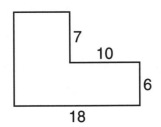

7
10
6
18

2. Perimeter: _____ units

Area: _____ units^2

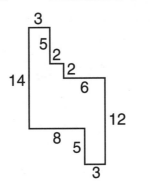

3
5
2
2
14
6
12
8
5
3

3. Perimeter: _____ units

Area: _____ units^2

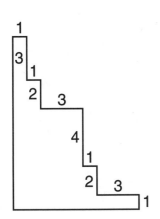

1
3
1
2
3
4
1
2
3
1

4. Perimeter: _____ units

Area: _____ units^2

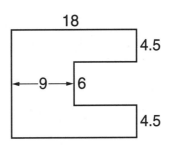

18
4.5
9
6
4.5

5. Perimeter: _____ units

Area: _____ units^2

2
2
1
2
1
4
5
3
1
3
2
2
2
2

Study Link 72: Finding Circumferences

The formula for the circumference of a circle is

Circumference = π * diameter or just **C = π * D**

Use the [π] key on your calculator to solve these problems. If your calculator doesn't have a [π] key, enter 3.14 each time you need π.

1. Find the circumference of each circle below. Show answers to the nearest tenth.

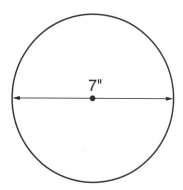

7"

6.4 cm

Circumference = _____ inches   Circumference = _____ centimeters

2. The wheels on Will's bicycle have a diameter of about 27", including the tire.

What is the circumference of the tire?

about _____ inches

About how far will Will's bicycle travel if the wheels go around exactly once?

about _____ inches

27"

3. Sofia measured the circumference of her bicycle tire. She found it was 66". What is the diameter of the tire?

about _____ inches

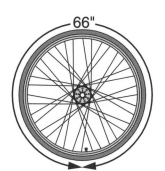

66"

Study Link 73: Measuring Land in Acres

In the United States, the acre is the most popular unit for measuring the size of a large piece of land. Small plots of land, such as average-size city lots, are usually measured in square feet instead of acres.

The drawing below shows a 1-square-mile area that has been divided into smaller pieces of land.

Find the number of acres in each piece of land. Write your answers on the drawing. (*Remember:* 1 square mile = 640 acres)

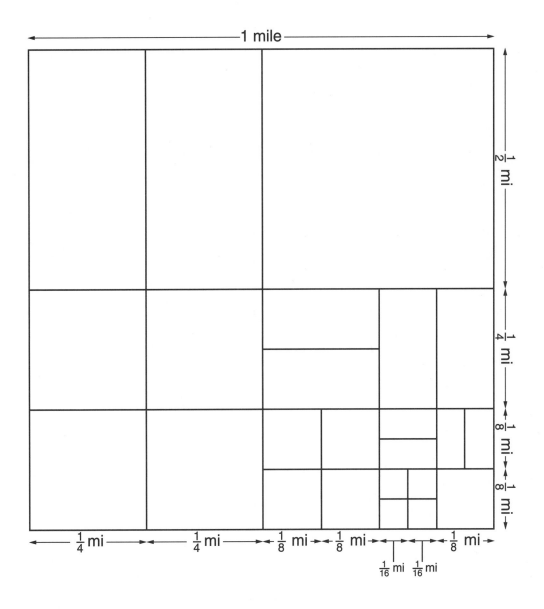

Study Link 74: Famous Large Buildings

The ground areas of buildings, their "footprints," are almost always given in square feet or square meters. Some buildings have very large ground areas. When their areas are given in square feet, the numbers are so large that it is hard to imagine how big the buildings really are.

Reference
1 acre = 43,560 square feet
For estimating, think of 1 acre as about 50,000 square feet.
A football field (excluding the end zones) is approximately 1 acre.

For large buildings, if you convert the area in square feet to an estimate in acres, you can get a better idea of the size of the building.

Estimate the ground area, in acres, of each building in the table below:

Example: The Colosseum, in Italy, covers an area of about 250,000 ft^2.
One acre is about 50,000 ft^2.
So 5 acres is about 250,000 ft^2.
The Colosseum covers an area of about 5 acres (5 football fields).

Building	Country	Date Built	Ground Area (ft^2)	Estimated Area (in acres)
Colosseum	Italy	70–224	250,000 ft^2	_5_ acres
Pyramid of Cheops	Egypt	c. 2600 B.C.	571,500 ft^2	_____ acres
Chartres Cathedral	France	1194–1514	60,000 ft^2	_____ acres
St. Peter's Basilica	Vatican City	1506–1626	392,300 ft^2	_____ acres
Taj Mahal	India	1636–1653	78,000 ft^2	_____ acres
Pentagon*	U.S. (Virginia)	1941–1943	1,263,000 ft^2	_____ acres
Ford Parts Center**	U.S. (Michigan)	1936	2,800,000 ft^2	_____ acres

*World record for ground area of an office building
**World record for ground area of one building

Study Link 75: Unit 7 Review

1. Find the areas of the figures below. Use formulas or some other methods.

Area of rectangle = length of base * height	$A = b * h$
Area of triangle = $\frac{1}{2}$ * length of base * height	$A = \frac{1}{2} * b * h$

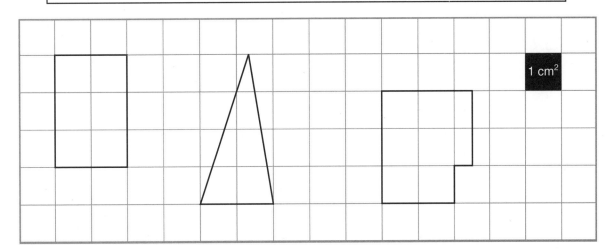

Area: _____cm²   Area: _____cm²   Area: _____cm²

2. Plot points B through J on the grid. Point A, (2,1), is plotted for you. Draw line segments to connect point A to point B, B to C, and so on. Connect J to A.

A	(2,1)	F	(5,4)
B	(3,3)	G	(6,4)
C	(2,4)	H	(5,3)
D	(3,4)	I	(6,1)
E	(4,5)	J	(4,2)

Describe the resulting shape.

_____

Is this shape a polygon? _____

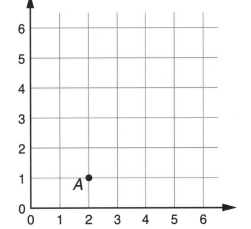

3. On the back of this paper, use your ruler to draw a rectangle that has an area of about 4 square inches and a perimeter of about 10 inches. Label each side with its length.

Hidden Treasure Gameboards

Grid 1

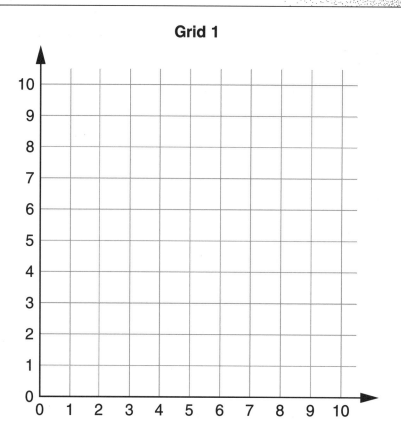

Grid 2

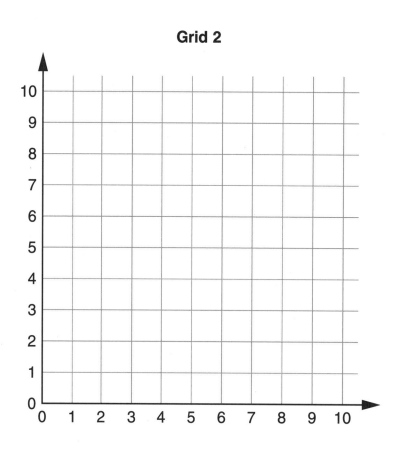

Latitudes

North

0° Latitude (Equator)	10°N	20°N	30°N	40°N
50°N	60°N	70°N		

South

0° Latitude (Equator)	10°S	20°S	30°S	40°S
50°S	60°S	70°S		

In squares for latitude, note that poles (90°N and 90°S) and latitudes 80°N and 80°S are not used.

Longitudes

0° Longitude (Prime Meridian)	10°W	20°W	30°W	40°W	50°W
60°W	70°W	80°W	90°W	100°W	110°W
120°W	130°W	140°W	150°W	160°W	170°W
180° Longitude	10°E	20°E	30°E	40°E	50°E
60°E	70°E	80°E	90°E	100°E	110°E
120°E	130°E	140°E	150°E	160°E	170°E

Study Link 64: Movie Theater Problem

Suppose you own a movie theater and need to decide which of two new movies to show.

You have done some research. The table at the right shows the number of people who saw the two movies at a theater like yours in another city over the weekend.

Tickets Sold

Day	*The Lost Elephant*	*Sir Isaac*
Friday	254	547
Saturday	878	636
Sunday	728	473

1. How many people saw each movie?

     a. *The Lost Elephant* _____   **b.** *Sir Isaac* _____

You also found that *The Lost Elephant* was seen by more children and *Sir Isaac* by more adults. One out of 2 people who saw *Sir Isaac* was an adult. Only 1 out of 4 people who saw *The Lost Elephant* was an adult.

2. How many adults and children saw each movie?

     a. *The Lost Elephant*   adults _____   children _____

     b. *Sir Isaac*   adults _____   children _____

3. At your theater, you charge $3 for a child's ticket and $6 for an adult's ticket. If approximately the same numbers and ratios of people saw the movies in your theater as in the theater above, about how much money would each movie make?

     a. *The Lost Elephant* $ _____   **b.** *Sir Isaac* $ _____

4. Which movie would you show and why?

     _____

     _____

Challenge

5. How many more people (adults and/or children) would have to see *The Lost Elephant* in a weekend to bring in more money than *Sir Isaac*?

     _____

     _____

Study Link 65: Converting Moneys

Mrs. Johns is planning a trip to India and has questions about the amount of money she will need. The current exchange rate is 38.34 Indian rupees to 1 U.S. dollar.

1. Complete the table at the right.

U.S. Dollars	Indian Rupees
$1.00	38.34
$1.50	
$10.00	
	600
$500.00	

2. Mrs. Johns's travel agent can get her a room at the New Delhi Hilton for 6000 rupees per night. How much is this in U.S. dollars?

3. Mrs. Johns plans to convert $550 into rupees. How many rupees will she get?

4. Mrs. Johns wants to find a mathematical formula so that she can mentally convert dollars to rupees and rupees to dollars without using a calculator. For each of the following, circle the rule that gives the best estimate.

a. Indian rupees =

    U.S. dollars + 40

    U.S. dollars − 40

    U.S. dollars * 40

    U.S. dollars / 40

b. U.S. dollars =

    Indian rupees + 40

    Indian rupees − 40

    Indian rupees * 40

    Indian rupees / 40

c. Explain why you chose your answers.

_____

_____

✔ Checking Progress

Individual Assessment

1. Use the graph at the right to answer the questions below.

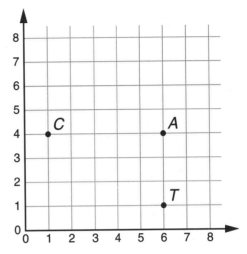

   a. What point has coordinates (1,4)?

   _____

   b. What are the coordinates of point *T*?

   _____

   c. Plot and label a point *S* on the graph so that polygon *CATS* is a rectangle. What ordered number pair names point *S?* _____

2. **a.** Plot and label the following points:

   A (1,1)   *B* (2,3)   *C* (5,3)   *D* (4,1)

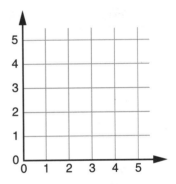

   b. Draw line segments to connect the points as follows:

   A to *B*, *B* to *C*, *C* to *D*, and *D* to *A*.

   c. Describe the figure you have drawn.

_____

_____

3. Each square in the grid at the right has an area of 1 cm². Mark and label a point *T* so that triangle *TRI* has an area of 5 cm².

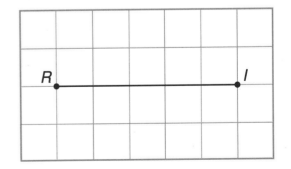

✔ **Checking Progress** (continued)

4. **a.** Measure the sides of the rectangle at the right to the nearest centimeter. Write the measurements on the sides. Include units.

b. What is the perimeter of the rectangle?

_____

c. What is the area of the rectangle? _____

5. Find the area of the figures below. Use the formulas to help you.

Area of a rectangle = length of base * height	$A = b * h$
Area of a parallelogram = length of base * height	$A = b * h$
Area of a triangle = $\frac{1}{2}$ * length of base * height	$A = \frac{1}{2} * b * h$

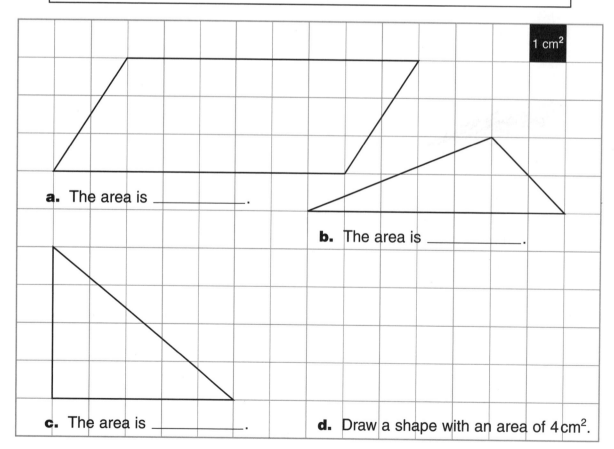

1 cm²

a. The area is _____.

b. The area is _____.

c. The area is _____.

d. Draw a shape with an area of 4 cm².

✓ Cumulative Review

1. Use your ruler. Measure the length and width of this page to the nearest $\frac{1}{2}$ inch.

   a. The length of this page

     is about _____ inches.

   b. The width of this page

     is about _____ inches.

2. **a.** In the space below, draw a line segment 5.5 cm long.

   b. This line segment is about

     _____ mm long.

3. Write the number 93 million with digits. _____

4. **a.** 150/9 → _____   **b.** $16\overline{)252}$ → _____

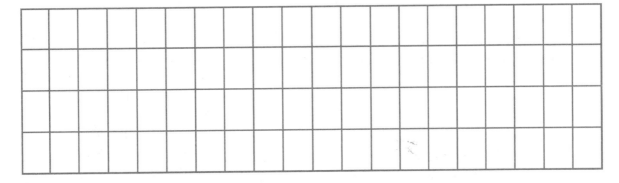

5. There are 58 fifth graders. Coach Swenson wants to put them in teams for the softball tournament.

   a. How many teams of 9 players can he form?

     _____

   b. How many teams of 11 players can he form?

     _____

   c. If he forms teams of 11 players, how many students will be left off a team?

     _____

6. I am a 5-digit number.
The digit in my tens place is 6.
The digit in my ten-thousands place is 5.
I have 2 hundreds.
I am divisible by 10.
The sum of all my digits is 14.
Write me below.

  ___ ___ , ___ ___ ___

Name _____   Name _____

Name _____   Name _____

Group Preassessment

1. Jim wants to build a fence around his rectangular garden. The garden is 15 feet by 5 feet.

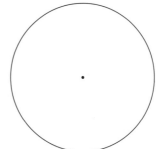

15 ft

5 ft

    a. In order to build a fence, does Jim need to find the area or the perimeter of the garden?

    _____

    b. What amount of fence does he need? _____

2.   **a.** What ordered number pair names point *A* in the coordinate grid at the right?

    _____

    b. Plot and label a point *C* in the grid so that triangle *ABC* has an area of 3 cm². What ordered number pair names point *C*?

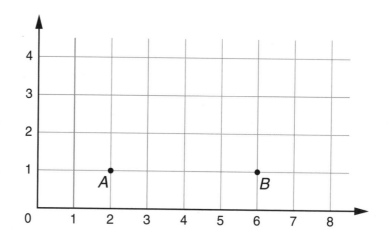

    _____

3. Measure the diameter of the circle at the right to the nearest centimeter.

    a. The diameter is about _____ cm.

    b. The radius is about _____ cm.

    c. The circumference is about _____ cm.

Circumference of a circle = π ∗ diameter

6. Complete each of the following sentences, rounding each answer to the nearest centimeter. Use the π key on your calculator or use 3.14 as an approximation for π.

> Circumference of a circle = π * diameter   Area of a circle = π * radius^2

a. The diameter is about _____ cm.

b. The radius is about _____ cm.

c. The circumference is about _____ cm.

d. The area is about _____ cm^2.

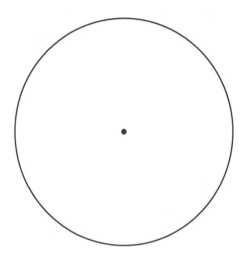

7. To solve each of the following problems, would you need to find the circumference, perimeter, or area? Circle the answer.

a. Mario ran around a circular track 20 times.
How far did he run?   circumference   area

b. Mr. Li is planting tomatoes in his garden.
He wants one plant for every 2 square feet.
How many plants should he buy?   perimeter   area

c. Jill is building a fence around her
rectangular lot. How many feet of
fencing should she buy?   perimeter   area

8. On the back of this paper, draw a rectangle with an area of 12 square inches and a perimeter of 16 inches.

Unit 8

Algebra Concepts & Skills

Study Link: Parent Letter

Unit 8: Algebra Concepts and Skills

In Unit 8, your child will add and subtract positive and negative numbers using several strategies. For example, red and black counters will be used to represent negative and positive numbers, as well as to model addition and subtraction problems.

The counters are used to represent an account balance. The red counters (−$1.00) show what portion of the account is a debt, or "in the red," while the black counters (+$1.00) show the portion of the account that is "in the black." For example, there are several ways to show an account balance of +$5.00 using red and black counters. Possible solutions are 5 black counters and 0 red, 6 black and 1 red, 7 black and 2 red, and so on. To assist your child, you may want to explain how a checking or savings account works.

Additionally, your child will be introduced to solving simple equations with a pan balance, thus developing basic skills of algebra. For example, as illustrated on the balance below, if you remove 3 marbles from the left pan and 3 marbles from the right pan, the pans will still balance. Therefore, you know that one cube weighs the same as 11 marbles.

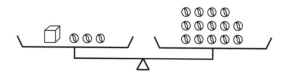

A "What's My Rule?" table has been a routine since the early grades of *Everyday Mathematics*. In this unit, your child will follow rules to complete tables, such as the one below. They will then graph the data. Your child will also determine rules from information provided in tables and graphs.

As the American Tour continues, your child will learn how to read, interpret, and design color-coded data maps. Additionally, students will work with variables and formulas when they visit Yellowstone National Park and learn how to predict eruption times of the famous geyser Old Faithful.

Rule

out = in + 4

in	out
1	5
2	
5	
	12
12	
	51

Study Link 77: Positive and Negative Numbers

1. Insert either a > (greater than) or a < (less than) symbol to make the following true.

     a. -7 _____ 6   **b.** 0.01 _____ -32

     c. 8.5 _____ -10^3 **d.** $-\frac{3}{4}$ _____ -1.6

2. Find the account balance. $\boxed{+}$ = $1 cash $\boxed{-}$ = $1 debt, or IOU

     a. Balance = $_____

     b. Balance = $_____

3. Solve these addition problems.

     a. $-15 + 6 =$ _____   **b.** $17 - (-5) =$ _____

     c. $-56 + (-32) =$ _____   **d.** $90 + (-20) =$ _____

     e. $18 + (-15) =$ _____   **f.** $-987 + 987 =$ _____

4. Use the rule to complete the table below.

in	out
15	5
300	
24	
1	
33	
102	

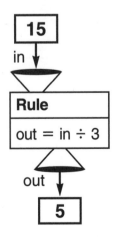

Study Link 78: How Likely Is Rain?

Many years ago, weather reports described the chances of precipitation with such phrases as "very likely," "unlikely," and "extremely unlikely." Nowadays, they are almost always reported as percents. For example, "There is a 50% chance of rain tonight."

1. Use the Probability Meter to translate phrases into percents.

Phrases	Percents
unlikely	*30%*
very likely	
very unlikely	
likely	
extremely unlikely	

2. Use the Probability Meter to translate percents into phrases.

Percents	Phrases
30%	*unlikely*
10%	
90%	
20%	
80%	
35%	
65%	
45%	

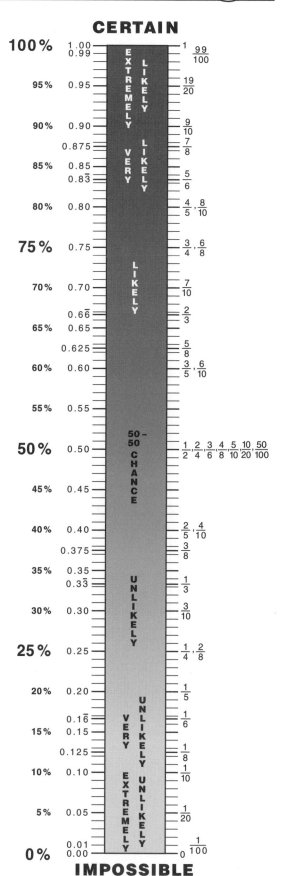

Study Link 79: Addition and Subtraction Problems

> **Reminder**
> To subtract a number, you can add the opposite of that number.

1. Solve each problem. *Be careful:* Some problems are additions; some are subtractions.

a. $-25 + (-16) =$ _____ **b.** $9.7 + (-6.7) =$ _____

c. $-4 - (-4) =$ _____ **d.** $-4 - 4 =$ _____

e. $29 - (-11) =$ _____ **f.** $-9 - (-11) =$ _____

g. $-100 + 15 =$ _____ **h.** $10 - 10.5 =$ _____

i. $0 - (-43) =$ _____ **j.** $4\frac{1}{2} + (-2\frac{1}{2}) =$ _____

k. $10 +$ _____ $= -5$ **l.** $10 -$ _____ $= 20$

2. In the table below, there are two number models in the "Temperature after Change" column. Only one of the number models in each row is correct. Complete the correct number model.

Temperature before Change	Temperature Change	Temperature after Change	
40°	up 7°	$40 + 7 =$ ____	$40 + (-7) =$ ____
10°	down 8°	$10 - (-8) =$ ____	$10 - 8 =$ ____
−15° (15° below zero)	up 10°	$-15 + 10 =$ ____	$15 + 10 =$ ____
−20° (20° below zero)	down 10°	$-20 + (-10) =$ ____	$20 - (-10) =$ ____

Study Link 80: Comparing Elevations

The number line below is marked to show the **elevation** of several well-known places.

Elevation is a measure of how far a location is above or below sea level. For example, an elevation of 5300 feet for Denver means that some point in Denver is 5300 feet above sea level. An elevation of −280 feet for Death Valley means that some point in Death Valley is 280 feet below sea level.

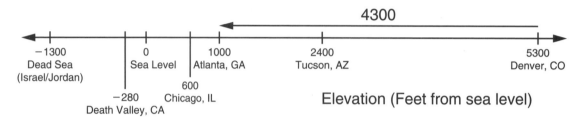

Fill in the table below. Use the example as a guide.

Example: If you start at Denver and travel to Atlanta, what is your change in elevation?

Solution: Draw an arrow above the number line. Start it at the elevation for Denver (5300 feet). End it at the elevation for Atlanta (1000 feet). Use the number line to find the length of the arrow (4300 feet). Your final elevation is lower, so report the change in elevation as 4300 feet down.

Start at	Travel to	Change in Elevation (up or down)
Denver	Atlanta	*4300* feet *down*
Chicago	Tucson	_____ feet _____
Death Valley	Dead Sea	_____ feet _____
Dead Sea	Death Valley	_____ feet _____
Tucson	Death Valley	_____ feet _____
Dead Sea	Atlanta	_____ feet _____

Study Link 81: Plotting Ordered Pairs

1. Plot the following ordered pairs on the grid below. As you plot each point, connect it with a line segment to the last one you plotted. (Use your ruler.)

$(0,3)$; $(3,-2)$; $(3,-8)$; $(-3,-8)$; $(-3,-2)$

2. Plot the following ordered pairs on the grid below. As you plot each point, connect it with a line segment to the last one you plotted. (Use your ruler.)

$(1,1)$; $(1,4)$; $(2,4)$

3. Plot the following ordered pairs on the grid below. As you plot each point, connect it with a line segment to the last one you plotted. (Use your ruler.)

$(1,-8)$; $(1,-5)$; $(-1,-5)$; $(-1,-8)$

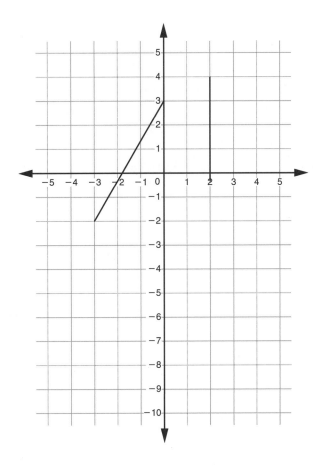

Study Link 82: Traveling on the Oregon Trail

On Saturday, April 9, 1853, Amelia Stewart Knight, her husband, and their 7 children left Monroe County, Iowa, and began a 2400-mile journey to Oregon. They arrived on September 17, 1853. In so doing, they joined one of the great migrations in U.S. history. Between 1840 and 1870, at least a quarter of a million people traveled from the banks of the Mississippi River to the West. Some went to claim free land in Oregon and California. Others hoped to make their fortune mining gold and silver.

1. About how many people traveled
   West between 1840 and 1870? _____

2. About how many months did it take
   Amelia Stewart Knight to reach Oregon? _____

By the time the Knight family struck out for Oregon, the trail was lined with the commerce of ferries, bridges, and supply stations. This made passage easier but also more expensive. It was common for a ferryman or bridge-keeper to charge travelers five dollars per wagon and fifty cents per head of oxen to cross a dangerous river.

Each family's covered wagon was typically driven by five oxen, and families often traveled in groups—or wagon trains—of 25 to 50 wagons.

3. About how much did it cost each
   family to cross a difficult river? _____

Challenge

4. About how much could a
   ferryman earn helping to move
   one wagon train across a river? _____

Source: *Women's Diaries of the Westward Journey.*

Study Link 83: Pan-Balance Problems

Solve these pan-balance problems. In each figure, the two pans are in perfect balance.

1. One △ weighs

   as much as _____ □.

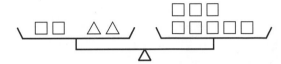

2. One cube weighs

   as much as _____ marbles.

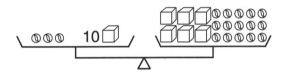

3. Two cantaloupes weigh

   as much as _____ apples.

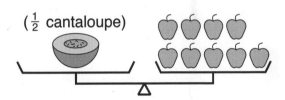

4. One *X* weighs

   as much as _____ *Y*.

5. One *B* weighs

   as much as _____ *M*.

Study Link 84: More Pan-Balance Problems

1. In each figure below, the two pans are in perfect balance. Solve these pan-balance problems:

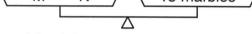

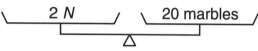

a. M weighs

as much as _____ marbles.

N weighs

as much as _____ marbles.

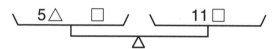

b. One △ weighs

as much as _____ □.

One □ weighs

as much as _____ marbles.

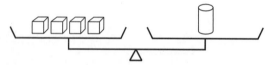

c. One can of juice weighs

as much as _____ blocks.

One apple weighs

as much as _____ blocks.

2. True or false?

a. (5 + 16) * 3 = 63 _____

b. 30 = ((9 + 7) − 1) * 2 _____

c. 38 = 2 + ((8 * 6) − 10) _____

d. 34 * (2 + 26) = 94 _____

3. Fill in the missing numbers to make true sentences.

a. _____ = (7 + 45)/2

b. ((28/7) + 12)/8 = _____

c. ((14 * 3) + 14) − 6 = _____

d. _____ = (3 − 3) * ((34/2) * 115)

Study Link 85: "What's My Rule?"

Complete each table according to the rule. Use a calculator if you wish.

1. Rule: Subtract 6 from the "in" number.

in	out
−5	
8	
10	
	−4
	−3

2. Rule: △ = 5 * □

□	△
4	
7	
6	
12	60
	6
	36

3. Rule: Add 7.5 to the "in" number.

in	out
−15	
37	
	4
−20	

4. Rule: △ = (9 * 7)/□

□	△
3	
2	
10	
	10.5
	63

Study Link 86: "What's My Rule?"

1. Complete each table below according to the rule.

a. Rule: Subtract the "in" number from 15.

in (n)	out (15 − n)
1	
2	
8	
	5
18	
	0

b. Rule: Triple the "in" number.

in (d)	out (3 * d)
7	
12	
	24
0.3	
	1
$\frac{1}{2}$	

c. Rule: Double the "in" number and add 3.

in (x)	out ((2 * x) + 3)
1	
2	
3	
	15
8	
	3

2. Complete each table below. Write the rule in words or as a formula.

3. Make up your own.

Challenge

a. Rule: _____

_____

_____

in	out
6	3
9	$4\frac{1}{2}$
1	0.5
12	
	8
4.40	

b. Rule: _____

_____

_____

in	out
1	1
2	3
3	5
4	
5	
	19

Rule: _____

_____

_____

in	out

Study Link 87: Cricket Formulas

In 1897, A. E. Dolbear, a physicist, published an article called "The Cricket as a Thermometer." In it he claimed that outside temperatures can be estimated by counting the number of chirps made by crickets and using the following formula:

$$\text{Outside temperature (°F)} = \frac{(\text{number of cricket chirps per minute} - 40)}{4} + 50$$

1. According to this formula, what is the estimated
outside temperature if you count 80 chirps in a minute?   _____

Other cricket formulas exist. This one is supposed to work particularly well
with field crickets:

$$\text{Outside temperature (°F)} = (\text{number of chirps in 15 seconds}) + 37$$

2. What outside temperature would be predicted
if you counted 35 chirps in 15 seconds?   _____

3. Compare the two formulas. If you counted 30 chirps in 15 seconds, what
temperature would each formula predict?

   a. First formula: _____

   b. Second formula: _____

4. Why might the type of cricket you are listening to affect the accuracy of
the prediction?

_____

_____

_____

_____

Source: *It's Raining Frogs and Fishes: Four Seasons of Natural Phenomena and Oddities of the Sky.*

Use with Lesson 87.   **Unit 8**

Study Link 88: Converting Celsius to Fahrenheit

In the U.S. customary system, temperature is measured in degrees Fahrenheit (°F). In the metric system, temperature is measured in degrees Celsius (°C). The temperature at which water freezes is 0°C, or 32°F.

You can use the following formula to convert temperatures measured in degrees Celsius to degrees Fahrenheit, where *F* stands for the number of degrees Fahrenheit and *C* for the number of degrees Celsius:

Formula: $F = (1.8 * C) + 32$

If you want to get a rough estimate of the temperature in degrees Fahrenheit, you can use the following rule of thumb:

Rule of thumb: Double the number of degrees Celsius and add the Fahrenheit freezing temperature.

$$F = (2 * C) + 32$$

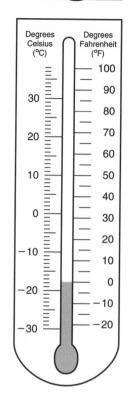

Convert the Celsius temperatures in the table to Fahrenheit temperatures, first using the formula and then the rule of thumb. Compare the results.

°C	−20	−10	0	10	20	30
°F (Use the formula.)						
°F (Use the rule of thumb.)						

Do you think that the results you get using the rule of thumb are close enough in most situations? _____

Explain. _____

_____

If you were sick and you took your temperature with a Celsius thermometer, would you use the formula or the rule of thumb to convert your temperature to degrees Fahrenheit? _____

Explain. _____

_____

Study Link 89: Mystery Graphs

Create a mystery graph on the grid below. Be sure to label the horizontal and vertical axes. Describe the situation that goes with your graph on the lines provided.

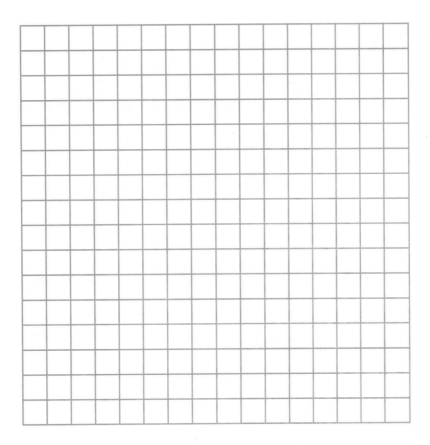

_____

_____

_____

_____

_____

_____

_____

_____

Use with Lesson 89.   **Unit 8**

Study Link 90: Review

1. Solve these addition and subtraction problems.

   a. −61 − (−21) = _____

   b. 90 − (−20) = _____

   c. −123 + (−56) = _____

   d. 1000 + (−1000) = _____

   e. −70 − 40 = _____

   f. −25 + 3 = _____

2. In each figure below, the two pans are in perfect balance. Solve these pan-balance problems:

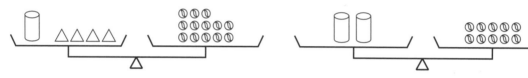

   a. One △ weighs as much

   as _____ marbles.

   One can weighs as much

   as _____ marbles.

   b. If the can is full, the water in the can weighs as much as _____ blocks.

   If the can is full, the water plus the can weigh as much as _____ blocks.

3. Using the table of x- and y-values below, mark each ordered number pair (x,y) as a point on the grid at the right.

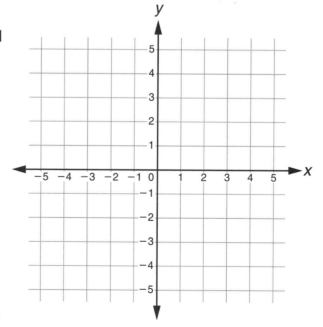

x	y
−1	−3
4	2
3	1
−3	−5
−2	−4

   What is the rule?

   _____

   _____

2-4-5-8-10 Frac-Tac-Toe (Bingo Version)

If you use a standard deck of playing cards:

- Use Queens as zeros (0).
- Use Aces as ones (1).
- Discard Jacks and Kings.

If you use an *Everything Math Deck,* discard cards greater than 10.

Fill in each gameboard by entering these numbers in the empty spaces:

0	0	0.2	0.25
0.3	0.4	0.5	0.5
0.6	0.7	0.75	0.8
1	1		

Numerator Pile

All remaining cards

Denominator Pile

Two each of 2, 4, 5, 8, and 10 cards

> 1.0		> 2.0		> 1.0
> 1.5	0.125 or 0.375	0.375 or 0.625	0.625 or 0.875	> 1.5
> 1.0		> 2.0		> 1.0

2-4-5-8-10 Frac-Tac-Toe (Bingo Version)

If you use a standard deck of playing cards:

- Use Queens as zeros (0).
- Use Aces as ones (1).
- Discard Jacks and Kings.

If you use an *Everything Math Deck,* discard cards greater than 10.

Fill in each gameboard by entering these numbers in the empty spaces:

0%	0%	20%	25%
30%	40%	50%	50%
60%	70%	75%	80%
100%	100%		

Numerator Pile

All remaining cards

Denominator Pile

Two each of 2, 4, 5, 8, and 10 cards

>100%		>200%		>100%
>150%	$12\frac{1}{2}\%$ or $37\frac{1}{2}\%$	$37\frac{1}{2}\%$ or $62\frac{1}{2}\%$	$62\frac{1}{2}\%$ or $87\frac{1}{2}\%$	>150%
>100%		>200%		>100%

Use with Lesson 85 and following.

✔ Cumulative Review

1. Circle all the numbers below that are greater than $\frac{1}{2}$.

$\frac{1}{4}$ $\frac{2}{3}$ 0.499 $\frac{3}{20}$ 0.090   1.5 $\frac{9}{100}$ $\frac{3}{5}$

2. What is another name for $\frac{3}{2}$?   _____

3. Mrs. Johnson has 8 grandchildren.

    a. Last week, Mrs. Johnson made $240 on a yard sale.
        She wants to give this money to her grandchildren
        so that each gets the same amount. How much will
        each child get?   _____

    b. On their birthdays, Mrs. Johnson gives each of her
        grandchildren $25 for their college savings accounts.
        How much does she spend on these birthday
        presents in a year?   _____

4. Use your ruler.

    a. Draw a line segment 5 inches long.

    b. Draw a line segment $2\frac{1}{2}$ inches long.

    c. Which of the line segments that you drew is
        closer in length to 8 centimeters?   _____

✔ Checking Progress

Preassessment

Work with the other members of your group.

1. Use your ⊞ and ⊟ counters to help solve the following problems:

   a. Mark has $8 dollars in cash. He also has debts
      of $15. Is he "in the red" or "in the black"?   _____

   b. What is his account balance?   _____

   c. Willie and Juan opened a lemonade stand.
      They spent $5 on supplies. On Friday they
      earned $3. On Saturday they earned $4.
      On Tuesday they earned $4. After expenses,
      how much did they earn?   _____

   d. Draw a picture of ⊞ and ⊟ counters
      that shows a balance of −$9.

   e. Draw a picture of ⊞ and ⊟ counters
      that shows a balance of $4. Use a
      total of 8 counters.

2. Mrs. Mauston rides her bike at an average
   speed of 8 miles per hour. Complete the
   table below. Then graph the data.

   Rule: Distance in miles = 8 ∗ time in hours

   a.

Time (hr)	Distance (mi)
1	8
2	_____
3	_____
3.5	_____
_____	48

   b.

   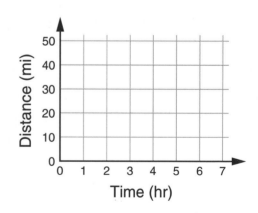

3. Louis used a pan balance. He found that it balanced
   if he put a pencil and 5 paper clips in one pan and
   23 paper clips in the other pan. About how many
   paper clips does the pencil weigh?   _____

✔ Checking Progress

1. Use your ⊞ and ⊟ counters.

  a. Draw a picture that shows an account with a balance of −$6.

  b. Draw a picture that shows a balance of $8, using exactly 10 counters.

  c. What is your balance if you have
the same number of ⊞ and ⊟ counters? _____

2. There are 15 ⊞ and 10 ⊟ counters in a box.

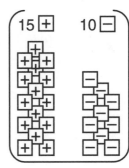

  a. What is the balance in the box? _____

  b. How many ⊟ counters do you need
to add to get a negative balance? _____

  c. What will be the new balance if you remove
6 ⊟ counters from the original balance? _____

  d. What will be the new balance if you:

    Remove 7 ⊟ counters from the original balance? _____

    Add 3 ⊟ counters to the original balance? _____

3. Solve. You may use your ⊞ and ⊟ counters or your slide rule to help you.

  a. $6 + (-8) =$ ____   **b.** $5 + (-2) =$ ____   **c.** $6 - (-5) =$ ____

  d. $-7 + 7 =$ ____   **e.** $8 + (-6) + (-8) =$ ____

4. Kerri is playing a game. She is 8 points "in the hole." (She has −8 points.)

  a. She gets 12 points on her next turn. What is her score now? _____

  b. If she loses 12 points instead, what will her score be? _____

5. Marge earns *D* dollars an hour.

a. Tom earns $5 an hour more than Marge. How much does he earn per hour? (Circle the answer.)

5 * *D*   *D* − 5   *D* + 5   *D* + *D*

b. Marge's aunt earns twice as much as Marge. How much does she earn per hour? (Circle the answer.)

2 * *D*   2 + *D*   *D* − 2 $\frac{1}{2}$ * *D*

c. Write an expression that shows how much Marge earns in 40 hours.

_____

6. The copy machine in the school office can make 40 copies per minute. This is given below as a rule.

a. Complete the table. Then graph the data in the table.
Rule: Number of copies = 40 * number of minutes

Time (min)	Number of Copies
1	_____
2	_____
_____	100
4	_____
_____	200

b. Ms. Southern needs to make 150 copies. About how long will this take?

_____

7. Mike drew the number line below. He made some mistakes. Cross out his mistakes and correct them.

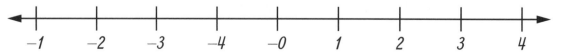

−1   −2   −3   −4   −0   1   2   3   4

✔ **Checking Progress** (continued)

8. Solve the pan-balance problems below.

a. One apple weighs

as much as _____ marbles.

b. One block weighs

as much as _____ marbles.

c. One ball weighs

as much as _____ blocks.

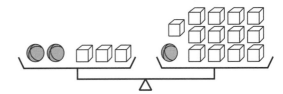

9. Shawna wrote an equation but covered one number.
$15 + 7 = \blacksquare + 12$. What is the covered number? _____

Challenge

10. Pete set up a pan balance. He found that 2 calculators balance 16 marbles. He then used the pan balance and found that 5 marbles balance 3 marbles and 10 paper clips. Fill in the blanks below.

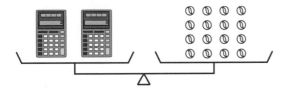

One calculator weighs

as much as _____ marbles.

One calculator weighs

as much as _____ paper clips.

Unit 9

Fractions & Ratios

Study Link: Parent Letter

Unit 9: Fractions and Ratios

In Unit 4, your child reviewed equivalent fractions and developed multiplication and division rules for finding equivalent fractions.

In this unit, your child will apply this knowledge to operations with fractions and mixed numbers. First, the class will explore addition and subtraction on a fraction slide rule similar to the slide rule students used for addition and subtraction of integers.

Second, the familiar clock face will be used to help find equivalent fractions and further explore addition and subtraction of fractions. Then a simple manipulative—fraction strips—will be used to find common denominators and assist in the development of algorithms for adding fractions with unlike denominators.

To prepare students for working with ratios in algebra, the class will review uses of fractions, including solving number stories involving ratios of part of a set to the whole set. Your child will find, write, and solve many number models.

The American Tour continues as your child reads an article about school attendance over the past 200 years in the *American Tour Almanac*. Based on the essay, students answer questions that require them to interpret information from tables, line graphs, and bar graphs. In another activity, students will compare their skills to those of students from previous generations by solving a series of problems that illustrates the changing emphases in mathematics instruction.

The class also reviews a political map of the United States and the electoral college. Students play *Algebra Election* to gain experience solving a variety of algebraic equations. Your child also plays *Build-It* and *Fraction Action, Fraction Friction* to practice sorting fractions and adding fractions with unlike denominators.

Finally, students will participate in a data exploration where they will gather, analyze, and graph their data, thus providing additional opportunities to explore fractions, ratios, and percents.

Use before or with Lesson 92.

Study Link 92: Line Segments

1. Draw a line segment approximately $3\frac{3}{8}$ inches long.

   If you made this line segment $\frac{1}{8}$ inch longer at
   each end, how long would the new segment be?
   (*Hint:* Use your ruler to figure this out.)   _____ in

   If you removed $\frac{1}{4}$ inch from one end of the
   original line segment, how long would the
   new segment be?   _____ in

2. Draw a line segment approximately $1\frac{15}{16}$ inches long.

   About how long is this line segment, to the
   nearest inch?   _____ in

   About how long is the line segment, to the
   nearest one-half inch?   _____ in

3. Which is longer, the line segment you drew in Problem 2
   or a line segment that is $1\frac{7}{8}$ inches long?

   _____

   By how much?   _____ in

4. Which is longer, the line segment you drew in Problem 1
   or a line segment that is $3\frac{6}{16}$ inches long?

   _____

   By how much?   _____ in

Study Link 93: Fraction Problems

1. To maintain their energy during the racing season, professional bicycle racers eat between 6000 and 8000 calories per day.

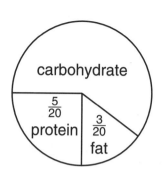

About $\frac{3}{20}$ of these calories come from fats, about $\frac{5}{20}$ come from proteins, and the remaining come from carbohydrate.

What fraction of a bicycle racer's calories comes from carbohydrate? _____

2. Study the plan for a small bookcase, shown at the right. All boards are $\frac{3}{4}$ inch thick.

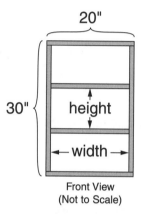

What is the width of each shelf? _____ inches

If the shelves are evenly spaced, what is the height of the opening for each of the 3 spaces? _____ inches

Front View
(Not to Scale)

3. Each square in the grid at the right represents a city block. Each side of a block is $\frac{1}{8}$ mile long, that is, in this city there are 8 blocks to each mile.

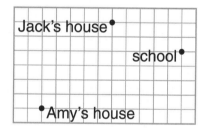

The distances below are measured along the sides of blocks.

a. The distance from Amy's house to school is

_____ blocks, or _____ mile(s).

b. The distance from Jack's house to school is

_____ blocks, or _____ mile(s).

c. How much farther from school is Amy's house than Jack's house? _____ mile(s)

d. Amy walks from school to Jack's house and then home. How far is that? _____ mile(s)

Study Link 94: Fraction Problems

Multiplication Rule for Finding Equivalent Fractions

To get an equivalent fraction, you can multiply both the numerator and the denominator of a fraction by the same number.

$$\frac{a}{b} = \frac{a * n}{b * n}$$

Example $\frac{4}{9} - \frac{1}{3} = ?$

$\frac{1}{3} = \frac{2}{6} = \frac{3}{9}$

Both fractions can be written with the common denominator 9.

$\frac{4}{9} - \frac{1}{3} = \frac{4}{9} - \frac{3}{9} = \frac{1}{9}$

Example $\frac{5}{8} + \frac{2}{5} = ?$

$\frac{5}{8} = \frac{10}{16} = \frac{15}{24} = \frac{20}{32} = \frac{25}{40} = \frac{30}{48}$

$\frac{2}{5} = \frac{4}{10} = \frac{6}{15} = \frac{8}{20} = \frac{10}{25} = \frac{12}{30} = \frac{14}{35} = \frac{16}{40} = \frac{18}{45}$

Both fractions can be written with the common denominator 40.

$\frac{5}{8} + \frac{2}{5} = \frac{25}{40} + \frac{16}{40} = \frac{41}{40}$ (or $1\frac{1}{40}$)

---

1. Find a common denominator. Then add or subtract.

   a. $\frac{2}{3} + \frac{4}{5} =$ _____

   b. $\frac{8}{9} - \frac{5}{6} =$ _____

   c. $\frac{3}{4} + 1\frac{1}{2} =$ _____

2. Lisa was 4 feet $10\frac{1}{2}$ inches tall at the end of 5th grade. During the year, she had grown $2\frac{3}{4}$ inches. How tall was Lisa at the start of 5th grade? _____

3. Bill was baking two different kinds of bread. One recipe called for $3\frac{1}{2}$ cups of flour, and the other called for $2\frac{1}{3}$ cups of flour. How much flour did Bill need? _____

Use with Lesson 94.   **Unit 9**

Study Link 95: Fraction Problems

1. Find a common denominator. Then add or subtract.

    a. $\frac{9}{11} - \frac{1}{2} =$ _____

    b. $\frac{5}{9} - \frac{1}{4} =$ _____

    c. $\frac{7}{10} + \frac{4}{15} =$ _____

    d. $\frac{7}{10} - \frac{4}{15} =$ _____

    e. $\begin{array}{r} \frac{3}{2} \\ - \frac{4}{9} \\ \hline \end{array}$

    f. $\begin{array}{r} \frac{5}{6} \\ + \frac{4}{7} \\ \hline \end{array}$

2. Write the fraction represented by the shaded part of each stick.

    a.  _____

    b.  _____

    c.  _____

    d.  _____

    e.  _____

    f. The sum of the five fractions in Parts 2a–2e is _____.

3. Use the information on Elise's shopping list to fill in the blanks below.

    a. Elise plans to buy _____ pounds of meat.

    b. She also plans to buy _____ pounds of cheese.

> **Elise's Shopping List**
> $\frac{1}{2}$ pound ham
> $\frac{3}{4}$ pound roast beef
> $\frac{2}{3}$ pound turkey
> $\frac{2}{3}$ pound Swiss cheese
> $\frac{1}{4}$ pound Parmesan cheese
> $\frac{2}{3}$ pound cheddar cheese

Study Link 96: More Fraction Problems

1. Circle all the fractions below that are greater than $\frac{3}{4}$.

$\frac{4}{5}$ $\frac{13}{20}$ $\frac{1}{2}$ $\frac{18}{25}$ $\frac{9}{12}$ $\frac{155}{200}$ $\frac{7}{11}$

2. Decide whether the sum or difference is greater than $\frac{1}{2}$, less than $\frac{1}{2}$, or equal to $\frac{1}{2}$. Circle your answer.

(*Hint:* Find a common denominator for each problem.)

a. $\frac{1}{10} + \frac{2}{7}$ $> \frac{1}{2}$ $< \frac{1}{2}$ $= \frac{1}{2}$

b. $\frac{5}{6} - \frac{1}{4}$ $> \frac{1}{2}$ $< \frac{1}{2}$ $= \frac{1}{2}$

c. $\frac{18}{20} - \frac{2}{5}$ $> \frac{1}{2}$ $< \frac{1}{2}$ $= \frac{1}{2}$

d. $\frac{3}{4} - \frac{1}{3}$ $> \frac{1}{2}$ $< \frac{1}{2}$ $= \frac{1}{2}$

3. Fraction Puzzle

Goal: To select and place three different numbers so that the sum is as large as possible.

Procedure: Select three different numbers from this list: 1, 2, 3, 4, 5, 6.

Write the same number in each square.

Write a different number in the circle.

Write a third number in the diamond.

Add the two fractions.

Example: If = 2, = 3, and ◯ = 4, then the sum is 2.

Study Link 97: Factor Trees

1. Make factor trees for the following numbers. An example has been done for you.

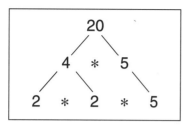

    a.   30   **b.**   45

2. Write each fraction in simplest form. Use factor trees to help.

    a. $\frac{20}{30} =$ _____   **b.** $\frac{20}{45} =$ _____   **c.** $\frac{30}{45} =$ _____

3. Find the prime factorization for 250. _____

4. **a.** Circle the number below that has the most prime factors. (You can use factor trees to help you.)

        63   32   49   100

    b. Which has the fewest prime factors? _____

Challenge

5. Simplify the fraction below. Use factor trees or some other method.

    $\frac{150}{225} =$ _____

Study Link 98: Fraction Problems

1. Dogs are owned by $36\frac{1}{2}$ percent of households in the United States. Birds are owned by $5\frac{7}{10}$ percent of households in the United States. What is the difference in percent of those households owning dogs and those owning birds? _____ %

2. The length of a typical blue whale is about $33\frac{1}{2}$ meters. The length of a typical pilot whale is about $6\frac{2}{5}$ meters. About how much longer is a blue whale? _____ m

3. President Bill Clinton is 6 feet $2\frac{1}{2}$ inches tall. The tallest President, Abraham Lincoln, was 6 feet 4 inches tall. What is the difference in these Presidents' heights? _____ in

4. In 1978, Penny Lee Dean of the United States became the fastest person ever to swim across the English Channel. Her time was $7\frac{2}{3}$ hours. The second fastest time was $7\frac{11}{12}$ hours by Philip Rush of New Zealand. How much faster did Dean complete the swim than Rush? _____ hr

5. In 1993, $\frac{2}{5}$ of the energy used in the United States came from petroleum, $\frac{1}{4}$ came from natural gas, and $\frac{23}{100}$ came from coal. The remaining energy came from hydropower and nuclear power. What fraction of the energy used in the United States was from hydropower and nuclear power? _____

6. A Major-League baseball bat cannot be larger than $2\frac{3}{4}$ inches in diameter or longer than 42 inches. Little-league bats cannot be larger than $2\frac{1}{4}$ inches in diameter or longer than 33 inches. What is the difference in maximum diameter between a Major-League and a little-league bat? _____ in

   What is the difference in maximum length? _____ in

Sources: *The World Almanac for Kids 1996; The Top 10 of Everything.*

Study Link 99: Ratio Problems

1. Draw a picture of 20 tiles so that 2 out of 10 tiles are white and the rest are shaded.

    a. How many tiles are white?   _____ tiles

    b. How many tiles are shaded?   _____ tiles

2. Draw 9 shaded tiles.

    Add some white tiles so that 2 out of 5 tiles are white.

    How many tiles are there in all?   _____ tiles

3. Imagine 48 tiles. If 4 out of 12 are white, how many are white?   _____ tiles

4. There are 24 players on the soccer team. Two out of every 3 players have not scored a goal yet this year. How many players have scored goals for the team?   _____ players

5. For every 8 spelling tests Justine took, she earned 3 perfect scores. If Justine earned 12 perfect scores this year, how many spelling tests did she take?   _____ tests

6. Make up and solve your own ratio number story. Be prepared to share it with the class.

    _____

    _____

    _____

    _____

    Answer: _____

✔ Cumulative Review

MASTER
70

1. The line segment below is $3\frac{1}{4}$ inches long. If you erased $1\frac{1}{2}$ inches from it, how long would the remaining line segment be?

_____ in

_____

2. **a.** On the line segment below, mark and label point B so that line segment AB is $2\frac{1}{8}$ inches long.

  b. On the line segment below, mark and label point C to the right of point B so that line segment BC is $1\frac{1}{4}$ inches long.

•_____

A

  c. How long is segment AC?

_____ in

3. As part of a school project, Joe found the following prices for a can of Super-Cola at nine different stores:

25¢, 31¢, 30¢, 39¢, 25¢, 42¢, 29¢, 25¢, 35¢

  a. What is the range of these prices?

_____

  b. What is the median price?

_____

  c. Is there a mode in this data set?

_____

    If yes, what is it?

_____

4. Make up a data set that has the following properties:

It has 7 numbers.   The median is 12.

The maximum is 20.   The range is 18.

Data set: _____

✔ Checking Progress

1. **a.** In the fraction $\frac{3}{10}$, the number 3 is called the _____ of the fraction.

   b. In the fraction $\frac{3}{10}$, the number 10 is called the _____ of the fraction.

   c. Write the decimal name for $\frac{3}{10}$. _____

2. In each of the following, complete the fractions so that they are equivalent.

   a. $\frac{4}{7} = \frac{\boxed{}}{14} = \frac{\boxed{}}{21}$

   b. $\frac{1}{4} = \frac{\boxed{}}{8} = \frac{8}{\boxed{}} = \frac{\boxed{}}{100}$

   c. What is a common denominator for $\frac{1}{4}$ and $\frac{4}{7}$? _____

3. Is $\frac{13}{25}$ greater than or less than $\frac{1}{2}$? _____

   Explain how you decided on your answer. _____

   _____

4. **a.** Use your ruler to draw a line segment $2\frac{3}{8}$ inches long.

   b. If you erased $\frac{3}{4}$ inch from this line segment, how long would the new line segment be? _____ in

   c. If you drew a line segment twice as long as the original ($2\frac{3}{8}$ in) line segment, how long would the new line segment be? (Circle one.)

   $4\frac{6}{16}$ in $4\frac{3}{4}$ in $4\frac{3}{8}$ in $4\frac{3}{16}$ in

5. Add or subtract.

   a. $5/8 + 3/8 =$ _____

   b. $\frac{3}{4} + 1\frac{1}{2} =$ _____

   c. $1 - \frac{2}{3} =$ _____

   d. $5/8 - 1/8 =$ _____

   e. $\begin{array}{r} 3\frac{1}{2} \\ + 1\frac{1}{8} \\ \hline \end{array}$

   f. $\begin{array}{r} 2\frac{3}{8} \\ - 1\frac{1}{2} \\ \hline \end{array}$

✔ Checking Progress (continued)

6. Write each fraction below in simplest form.

a. $\frac{4}{20}$ = _____

b. $\frac{18}{24}$ = _____

c. $\frac{28}{24}$ = _____

7. Tyrone is baking bread. The recipe calls for $\frac{3}{4}$ cup of whole-wheat flour and $1\frac{1}{2}$ cups of white flour. How much flour is used in all?

_____ cups

8. Bobbie measured the growth of her corn plant every week. One Friday, it was $3\frac{7}{8}$ inches tall. The following Friday, it was $6\frac{3}{4}$ inches tall. How much had it grown?

_____ in

9. How many minutes are there in $\frac{1}{3}$ of an hour?

_____ min

10. After school, Juan spent $\frac{1}{3}$ of an hour reading and $\frac{1}{2}$ of an hour practicing the piano.

a. For how many minutes did he read and practice piano?

_____ min

b. What fraction of an hour is this? Circle the best answer below.

$\frac{5}{6}$ $\frac{2}{5}$ $\frac{2}{6}$ $\frac{6}{5}$

11. Mary Lou baked 36 cupcakes for the bake sale. If $\frac{2}{3}$ of them had chocolate frosting, how many cupcakes had chocolate frosting?

_____ cupcakes

12. To celebrate doing well on their fraction test, Joe and Linda bought a pizza. Joe ate $\frac{1}{4}$ and Linda ate $\frac{1}{3}$ of the pizza.

a. What fraction of the pizza was left?

_____

b. The pizza was cut into slices of equal size. If each person ate only whole slices, into how many slices had the pizza been cut?

_____

Explain your answer. _____

_____

c. If you wanted to cut a pizza so that whole slices could be shared equally by 2 people, 3 people, 4 people, 6 people, or 8 people, into how many slices would you cut it?

_____ slices

Study Link 101: Unit 9 Review (continued)

9. Which cake below is sliced so that the whole cake can be shared equally among 3, 4, or 6 people? Circle the correct cake.

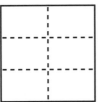 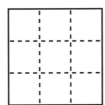 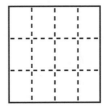

10. a. Use your ruler to draw a line segment $2\frac{1}{8}$ inches long.

b. Use your ruler to draw a line segment $1\frac{3}{16}$ inches long.

c. How much longer is the line segment in Part a than the line segment in Part b? _____ in

11. Is $\frac{1}{2} + \frac{1}{4} + \frac{1}{8} + \frac{1}{16}$ greater than 1 or less than 1? _____

Explain how you know. _____

_____

_____

_____

Electoral Vote Map (left)

MASTER
65

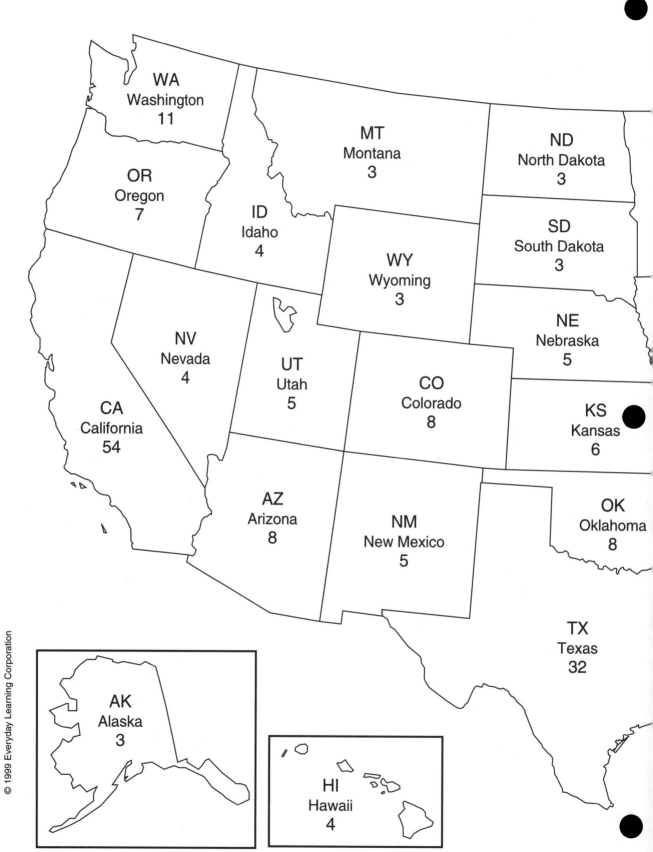

Use with Lesson 92 and following.

Unit 9

Electoral Vote Map (right)

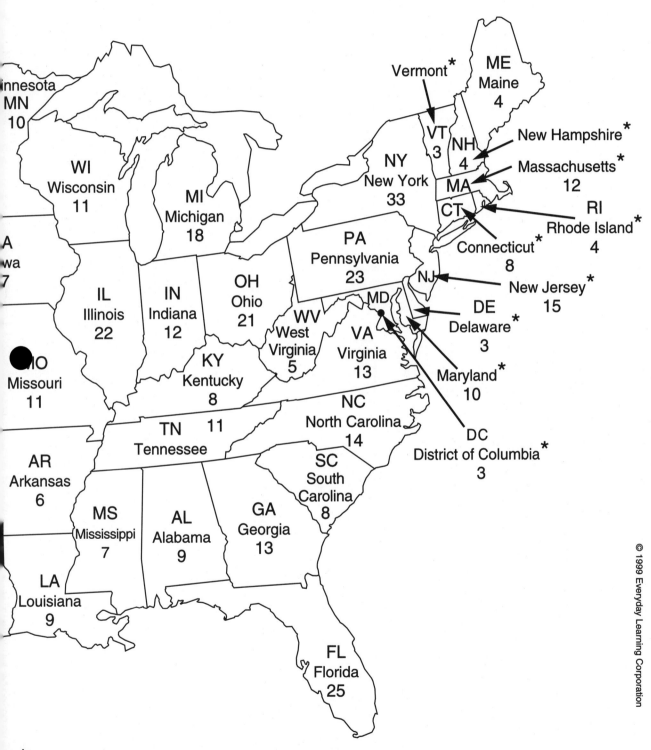

*If your marker does not fit on the state, put your marker on the state name.

Six-Inch Ruler

Not Actual Size

Slide Rule

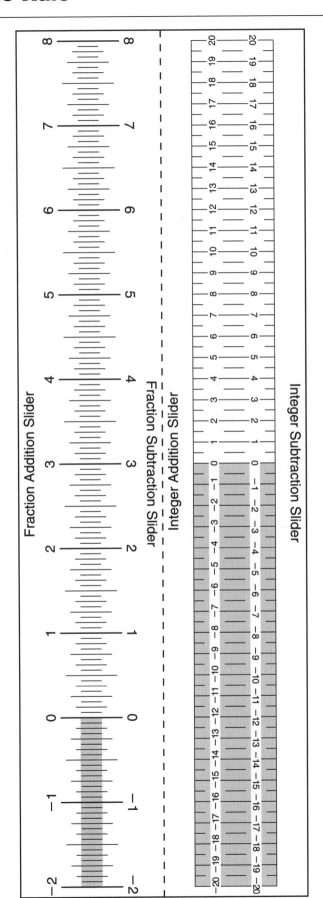

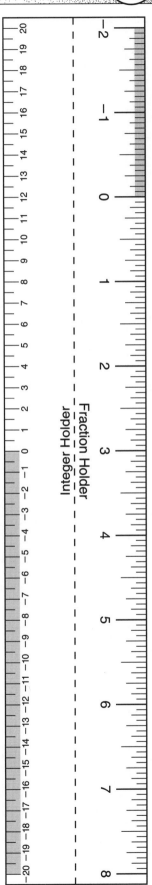

When Do Drivers Turn Their Headlights ON?

1	3:52 P.M.[2]	12	0
2	3:56	16	1
3	4:00	15	0
4	4:04	11	2
5	4:08	9	4
6	4:12	11	9
7	4:16	5	7
8	4:20	5	5
9	4:24	7	11
10	4:28	3	11
11	4:32	3	15
12	4:36	0	11
13	4:40	0	15
14	4:44	1	19
15	4:48[3]	0	15

1	3:52 P.M.[2]	12	0
2	3:56	16	1
3	4:00	15	0
4	4:04	11	2
5	4:08	9	4
6	4:12	11	9
7	4:16	5	7
8	4:20	5	5
9	4:24	7	11
10	4:28	3	11
11	4:32	3	15
12	4:36	0	11
13	4:40	0	15
14	4:44	1	19
15	4:48[3]	0	15

1	3:52 P.M.[2]	12	0
2	3:56	16	1
3	4:00	15	0
4	4:04	11	2
5	4:08	9	4
6	4:12	11	9
7	4:16	5	7
8	4:20	5	5
9	4:24	7	11
10	4:28	3	11
11	4:32	3	15
12	4:36	0	11
13	4:40	0	15
14	4:44	1	19
15	4:48[3]	0	15

1	3:52 P.M.[2]	12	0
2	3:56	16	1
3	4:00	15	0
4	4:04	11	2
5	4:08	9	4
6	4:12	11	9
7	4:16	5	7
8	4:20	5	5
9	4:24	7	11
10	4:28	3	11
11	4:32	3	15
12	4:36	0	11
13	4:40	0	15
14	4:44	1	19
15	4:48[3]	0	15

© 1999 Everyday Learning Corporation

Use with Lesson 101.

Unit 10

Volume

Study Link: Parent Letter

Unit 10: Volume

Unit 10 focuses on developing your child's ability to think spatially. Many times, students may feel that concepts of area and volume are of little use in their everyday lives as compared with their computation skills. Encourage your child to become more aware of the importance and relevance of two- and three-dimensional shapes. Point out geometric solids (such as pyramids, cones, and cylinders) as well as two-dimensional shapes (such as squares, circles, and triangles) in your surroundings.

Area is defined as the number of units (usually squares) that can fit into a bounded surface without gaps or overlaps. Your child will have an opportunity to review formulas for finding the area of a rectangle, parallelogram, and triangle. Your child will also explore the formula for finding the area of a circle. These formulas will later be used to calculate the surface area of three-dimensional shapes.

Volume (or capacity) is the measure of the amount of space inside a three-dimensional geometric figure. Your child will develop formulas to calculate the volume of rectangular and curved shapes.

This unit's goal is not to have the students memorize area and volume formulas, but rather to help them develop an appreciation for their use and application in various settings. By the end of this unit, your child will have had many experiences using two- and three-dimensional geometry.

Study Link 103: Cube Patterns

There are four patterns below. Three of the patterns can be folded to form a cube.

1. Try to guess which of the patterns cannot be folded into a cube.

My guess: Pattern _____ (A, B, C, or D) cannot be folded into a cube.

2. Cut and fold the pattern to check your guess. Did you make the correct guess?

If not, try other patterns until you find the one that does not form a cube.

My answer: Pattern _____ (A, B, C, or D) cannot be folded into a cube.

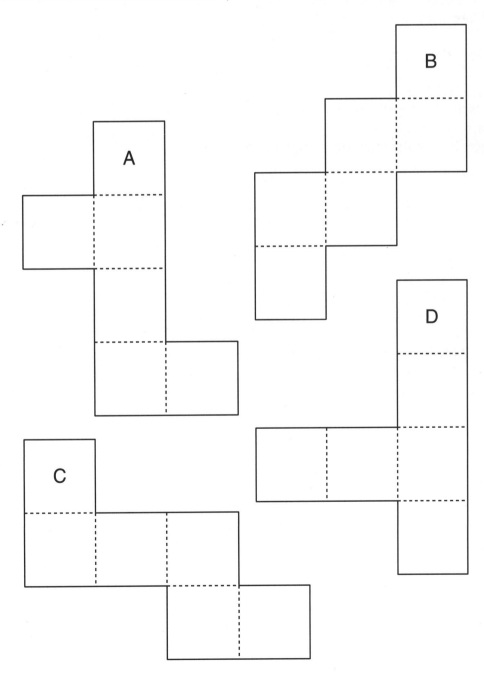

Use with Lesson 103.

Unit 10

Study Link 104: Faces, Vertices, and Edges

1. Refer to the pictures of polyhedrons on the next page to complete the following table:

Polyhedron	Number of Faces (f)	Number of Vertices (v)	Number of Edges (e)
Rectangular Prism	6		
Tetrahedron		4	
Triangular Prism			9
Rectangular Pyramid			
Octahedron			

2. Look for a pattern in the results in your table.

   a. If you know the numbers of faces and vertices in a polyhedron, how can you calculate the number of edges, without counting them?

   _____

   _____

   _____

   b. Express your calculation as a formula. Let f represent the number of faces, let v represent the number of vertices, and let e represent the number of edges in the polyhedron.

   $e =$ _____

   c. Check that this formula is true for other polyhedrons.

   This formula is sometimes called Euler's Formula, named after the 18th-century Swiss mathematician and physicist, Leonhard Euler.

Study Link 104: Faces, Vertices, and Edges (continued)

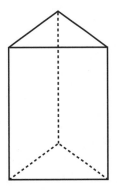

Triangular
Prism

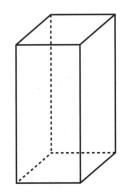

Rectangular
Prism

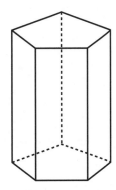

Pentagonal
Prism

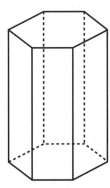

Hexagonal
Prism

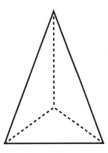

Triangular
Pyramid

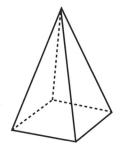

Rectangular (Square)
Pyramid

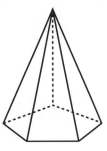

Pentagonal
Pyramid

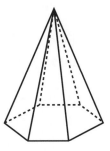

Hexagonal
Pyramid

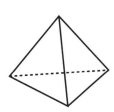

Tetrahedron

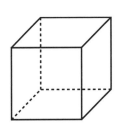

Cube

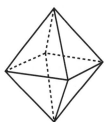

Octahedron

Study Link 105: Review of Two-Dimensional Figures

Match each description of a geometric figure in Column A with its name in Column B. Not every name in Column B has a match.

A

a. A polygon with 4 right angles and 4 sides of the same length

b. A polygon with 4 sides, no two of which need to be the same size

c. A quadrilateral with exactly one pair of opposite sides that are parallel

d. Lines in the same plane that never intersect

e. A parallelogram (that is not a square) with all sides the same length

f. A polygon with 8 sides

g. Two intersecting lines that form a right angle

h. A polygon with 5 sides

i. An angle that measures 90°

j. A triangle with all sides the same length

B

_____ octagon

_____ rhombus

_____ right angle

_____ acute angle

_____ trapezoid

_____ hexagon

_____ square

_____ equilateral triangle

_____ perpendicular lines

_____ parallel lines

_____ pentagon

_____ isosceles triangle

_____ quadrilateral

Study Link 106: Reasonable Measurements

1. For each statement below, write *S* if the measurement given is too small, *OK* if the measurement is reasonable, or *L* if the measurement is too large.

If the measurement given is too small or too large, supply a measurement that you think is reasonable.

a. _____ A full can of a soft drink holds about 350 milliliters of liquid.   _____

b. _____ A car's fuel tank holds approximately 500 liters of gasoline.   _____

c. _____ A person should drink about 2 liters of water each day.   _____

d. _____ The volume of your math journal is about 15 cubic centimeters.   _____

e. _____ The volume of a toaster is about 1 cubic foot.   _____

f. _____ An average fifth grader is approximately 1000 millimeters tall.   _____

2. Write three statements of your own, similar to those above. One statement should contain a measurement that is too small, one statement should contain a measurement that is reasonable, and the final statement should contain a measurement that is too large.

Too Small: _____

_____

Reasonable: _____

_____

Too Large: _____

_____

Study Link 107: A Volume Experiment

Part 1

Materials   ❑ an empty plastic soft-drink bottle

              ❑ a small wad of paper

Directions

- Place the empty plastic bottle on its side.

- Place the wad of paper in the neck.

- Try to blow the paper into the bottle.

1. Were you able to blow the paper into the bottle? _____

Instead of going into the bottle, the wad of paper probably flew back at you when you tried to blow it in. Before you blew into the bottle, there was the same amount of air per cubic inch inside the bottle as outside the bottle. When you blew into the bottle, you were putting more air into the bottle. As a result, the amount of air per cubic inch *inside* the bottle became greater than the amount of air per cubic inch *outside* the bottle. To put it another way, the air pressure inside the bottle became greater than the air pressure outside the bottle. In areas that are next to each other, air will always move to equalize pressure in the two areas. Therefore, some of the air in the bottle rushed out and carried the paper with it.

Part 2

Materials   ❑ same as above

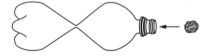

Directions

- Squeeze the bottle in the middle to make a dent.

- Hold the bottle horizontally and place the wad of paper in the neck.

- Squeeze the bottle to get rid of the dent.

2. Describe what happened to the paper. Why do you think this happened?

_____

_____

_____

Study Link 108: Sensible Statements

Do you think the following statement is true?

"There are more dogs than people in the United States."

If this statement were true, most families would have as many dogs as people, and some families would have more dogs than people. You probably know many families who have fewer dogs than people and many who have no dogs.

Tell whether you think each of the following statements is true or false. Circle T or F. Use mathematical evidence and your knowledge of the world to support your decisions. Write your reasons on the back of this paper.

1. "Most doors are about 12 feet tall." True or false?   T or F
What evidence do you have to support your position?

2. "A fifth grader usually spends between 30 and 40 hours a   T or F
week in school." True or false? What evidence do you
have to support your position?

3. "A typical house cat weighs as much as 50 pounds."   T or F
True or false? What evidence do you have to support
your position?

4. "The average fifth grader eats about 700 doughnuts   T or F
per year." True or false? What evidence do you have
to support your position?

5. "We spend about one-quarter to one-third of our lives   T or F
sleeping." True or false? What evidence do you have to
support your position?

Challenge

6. "The number of people in the United States whose   T or F
birthday is today is between 500 thousand and 1 million."
True or false? What evidence do you have to support
your position? (*Hint:* There are about 260 million people
residing in the United States.)

Study Link 109: Volumes of Cylinders

Formula for the Volume of a Cylinder	Formula for the Area of a Circle
$V = B * h$	$A = \pi * r^2$
where V is the volume of the cylinder, B is the area of the cylinder's base, and h is the height of the cylinder.	where A is the area of the circle and r is the length of the radius of the circle.
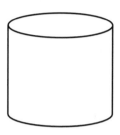	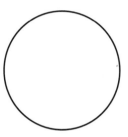

1. Find the smallest cylinder in your home. Record its dimensions and calculate its volume.

    Radius = _____   Height = _____

    Area of base = _____   Volume = _____

2. Find the largest cylinder in your home. Record its dimensions and calculate its volume.

    Radius = _____   Height = _____

    Area of base = _____   Volume = _____

3. Is the volume of the largest cylinder
    more or less than the volume of your toaster?   _____

    About how much more or less?   _____

4. Is the volume of the largest cylinder more or less
    than the volume of your television set?   _____

    About how much more or less?   _____

Use with Lesson 109.

Unit 10

Study Link 110: Review of Area

Area Formulas

Rectangle:	Parallelogram:	Triangle:
$A = b * h$	$A = b * h$	$A = \frac{1}{2} * b * h$

where A is the area, b is the length of the base, and h is the height.

---

1. Find the areas of rectangles with the following dimensions. Do not forget the units. You might want to make a sketch of the rectangles on a piece of scratch paper.

   a. Length of base = 8 in   Height = 15 in   Area = _____ _____

   b. Length of base = 19 cm   Height = 20 mm   Area = _____ _____

   c. Length of base = 18 in   Height = 3 ft   Area = _____ _____

2. Find the area of each of the polygons pictured below.

   a.

   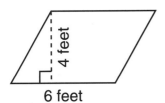

   4 feet

   6 feet

   Area = _____ _____

   b.

   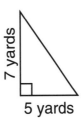

   7 yards

   5 yards

   Area = _____ _____

   c.

   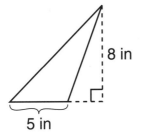

   8 in

   5 in

   Area = _____ _____

   d.

   6 cm

   2 cm

   Area = _____ _____

3. Use a dictionary to find the meaning(s) of each of the following words:

   a. displacement: _____

   _____

   b. calibrate: _____

   _____

Study Link 111: Cram-in-the-Cotton Experiment

Try this experiment at home.

Materials
- ❑ drinking glass
- ❑ water
- ❑ 2 large handfuls of cotton. (Be sure to use real cotton. Synthetic materials will not work.)

Directions

- Fill the drinking glass almost to the top with water.
- Put the cotton bit by bit into the glass. Fluff it as you go.

If you are careful, you should be able to fit all of the cotton into the glass without spilling a drop of water.

Think about what you know about displacement and volume. Why do you think you were able to fit the cotton into the glass without the water overflowing?

_____

_____

_____

_____

_____

_____

_____

_____

_____

_____

_____

_____

Study Link 112: Review

Use the formulas below to complete Problems 1–4. If your calculator at home does not have a [π] key, use 3.14 to approximate the value of π. Round all answers to the nearest tenths place.

Formulas

Area of circle = π * radius * radius

Volume of cylinder = Area of base * height

---

1. Find a cylinder in your house.

   a. What is your example of a cylinder? _____

   b. Estimate its volume. _____ cm³

2. Measure to the nearest 0.5 cm.

   a. What is the diameter of the base? _____

   b. What is the radius of the base? _____

3. What is the area of the base? _____

4. What is the volume of the cylinder? _____

5. A centimeter cube has a volume of 1 cubic centimeter. A typical die is slightly larger, nearly 2 cubic centimeters. A soft-drink can has a volume of about 350 cubic centimeters.

Use these measurements as a guide.

Find objects in your home with the following volumes:

   a. Less than 5 cubic centimeters: _____

   b. Between 100 and 500 cubic centimeters: _____

   c. More than 1000 cubic centimeters: _____

Cube Pattern

Cut on the solid lines.
Fold on the dashed lines.
Tape or glue the tabs "inside" or "outside" the figure.

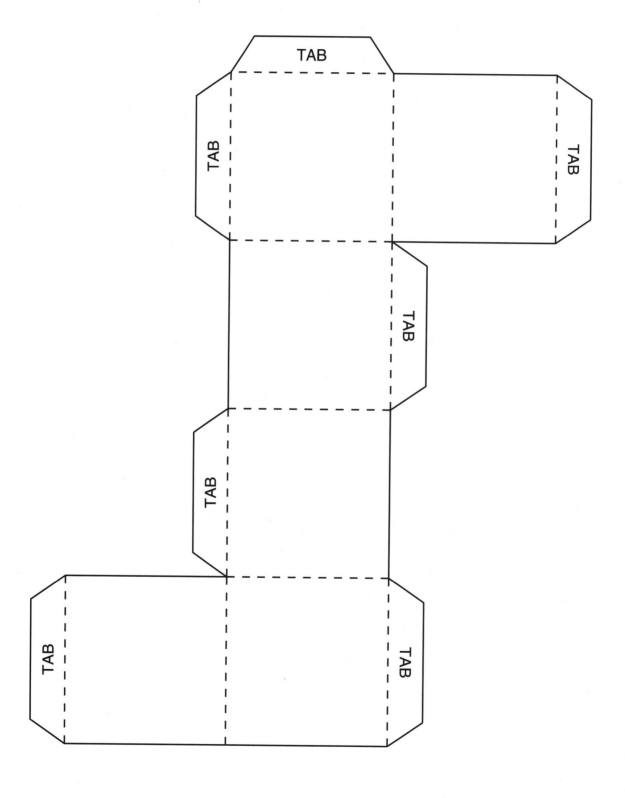

Study Link 114: Fractions of Fractions

Example:

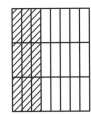 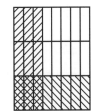

The whole rectangle represents ONE.

Shade $\frac{3}{8}$ of the interior.

Shade $\frac{1}{3}$ of the interior in a different way.

The double shading shows that $\frac{1}{3}$ of $\frac{3}{8}$ is $\frac{3}{24}$, or $\frac{1}{8}$.

In each of the following problems, the whole rectangle represents ONE.

1. Shade $\frac{3}{5}$ of the interior.

Shade $\frac{2}{3}$ of the interior in a different way.

The double shading shows that

$\frac{2}{3}$ of $\frac{3}{5}$ is _____.

2. Shade $\frac{3}{4}$ of the interior.

Shade $\frac{1}{3}$ of the interior in a different way.

The double shading shows that

$\frac{1}{3}$ of $\frac{3}{4}$ is _____.

Challenge

3. Shade $\frac{4}{5}$.

Shade $\frac{3}{4}$ of the interior in a different way.

The double shading shows that

$\frac{3}{4}$ of $\frac{4}{5}$ is _____.

4. Shade $\frac{5}{8}$.

Shade $\frac{3}{5}$ of the interior in a different way.

The double shading shows that

$\frac{3}{5}$ of $\frac{5}{8}$ is _____.

5. Tara has gone to the movie theater 20 times this year. Three-fourths of the movies she saw were comedies. Tara really enjoyed $\frac{3}{5}$ of the comedies she saw. How many comedies did she really enjoy this year? _____

6. Hiromitsu and Jina together ate 12 slices of pizza. One-third of these slices had pepperoni. One-fourth of the slices with pepperoni also had mushrooms. How many slices had both toppings? _____

Study Link 115: Multiplying Fractions

1. Write a number model for each area model.

   Example:

   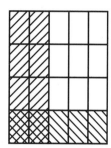   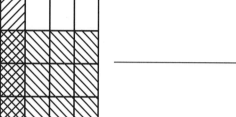   **a.** 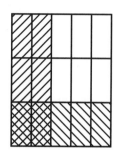 _____

   b. _____   **c.** _____

2. Multiply.

   a. $\frac{3}{7} * \frac{2}{10} =$ _____   **b.** $\frac{5}{6} * \frac{2}{3} =$ _____   **c.** $\frac{1}{2} * \frac{1}{4} =$ _____

   d. $\frac{4}{5} * \frac{3}{5} =$ _____   **e.** $\frac{2}{3} * \frac{3}{8} =$ _____   **f.** $\frac{1}{7} * \frac{5}{9} =$ _____

3. Matt is making cookies for the school fund-raiser. The recipe calls for $\frac{2}{3}$ cup of chocolate chips. He decides to triple the recipe. How many cups of chocolate chips does he need?

   _____ cups

4. The total number of goals scored by both teams in the field-hockey game was 15. Julie's team scored $\frac{3}{5}$ of the goals. Julie scored $\frac{1}{3}$ of her team's goals. How many goals did Julie's team score?

   _____ goals

   How many goals did Julie score?

   _____ goals

5. Girls are one-half of the fifth grade class. Two-tenths of these girls have red hair. Red-haired girls are what fraction of the fifth grade class?

   _____

Triangular Prism Pattern

Cut on the solid lines.

Fold on the dashed lines.

Tape or glue the tabs "inside" or "outside" the figure.

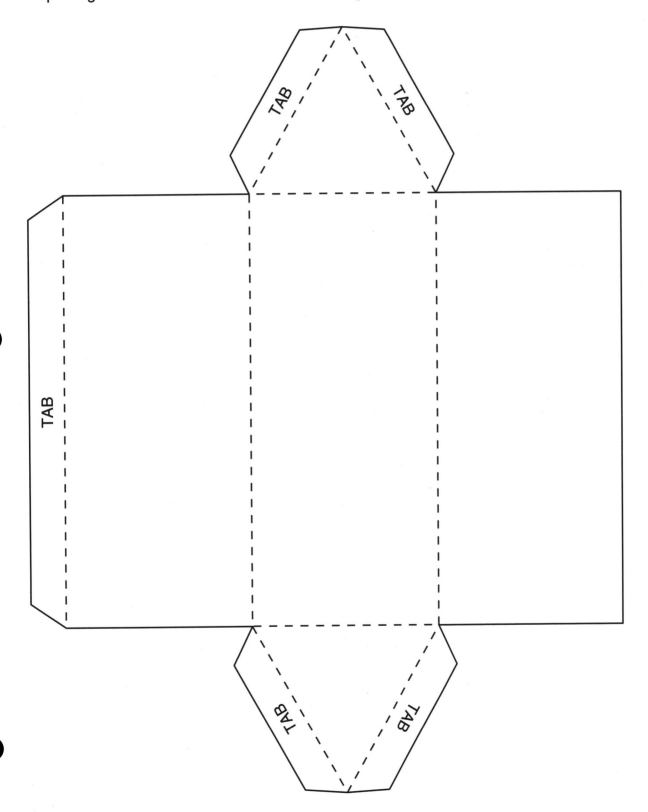

Use with Lesson 103.

Unit 10

Triangular Pyramid Pattern

Cut on the solid lines.
Fold on the dashed lines.
Tape or glue the tabs "inside" or "outside" the figure.

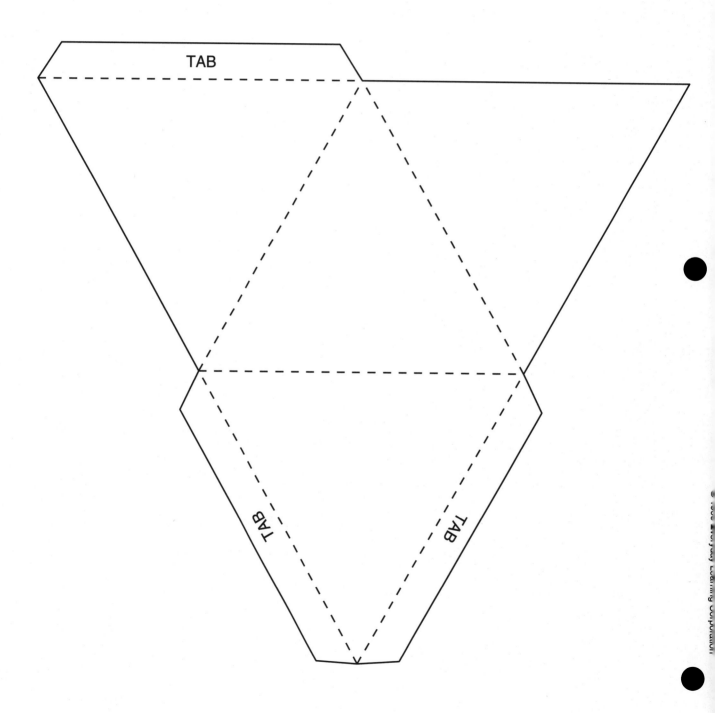

Use with Lesson 103.

Unit 10

Square Pyramid Pattern

Cut on the solid lines.

Fold on the dashed lines.

Tape or glue the tabs "inside" or "outside" the figure.

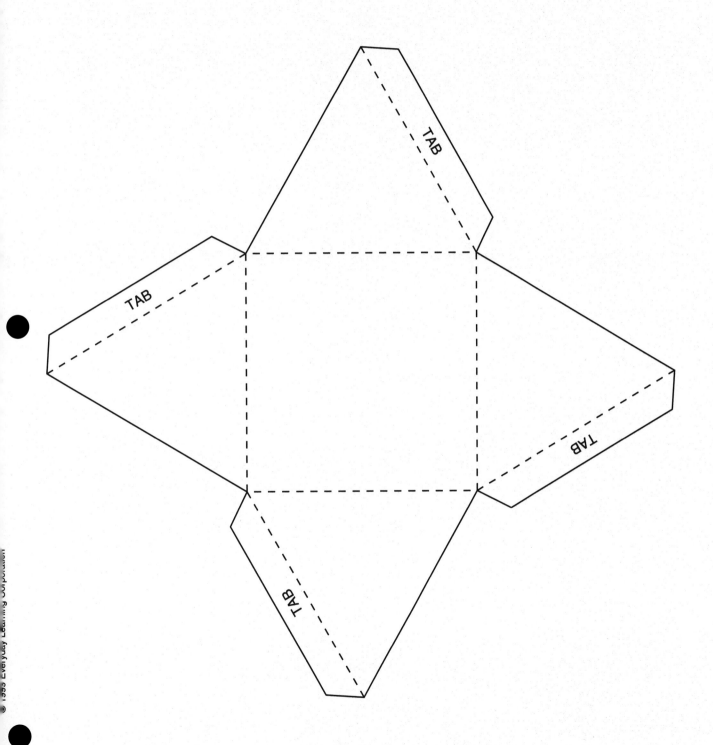

Venn Diagram

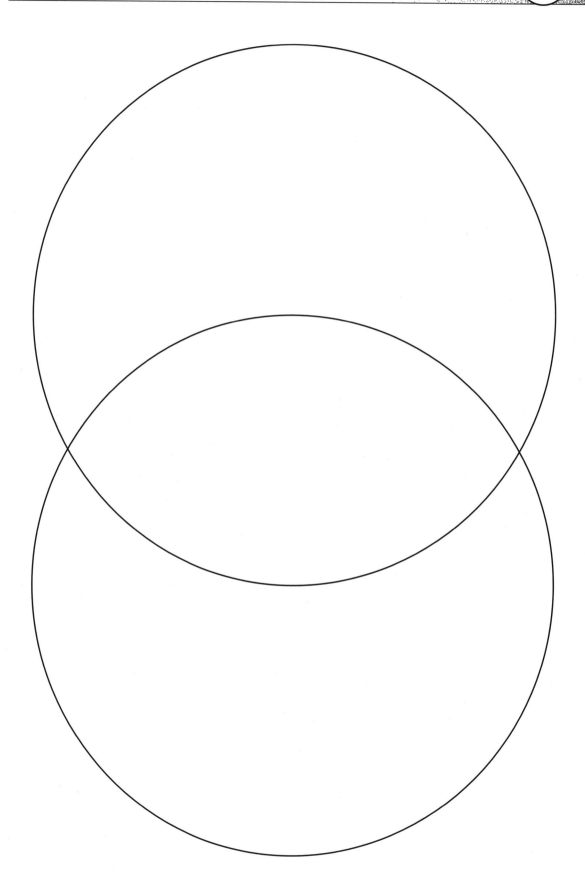

Use with Lesson 104.

Unit 10

Making a 50-mL Measuring Cone

Cut out one of the cone templates from Activity Sheet 24 and attach a strip of tape on the back side, as shown.

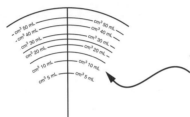

Curl the cone into position, lining up the two heavy black lines and the sets of blue lines.

While one partner holds the top edge in position, the other partner pulls the tape to make the lines come together at the apex (tip) of the cone. When all the lines are in the right position, press the tape down, and then use more tape to seal the seams on the inside and outside so that your cone won't leak.

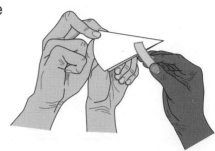

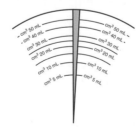

This is how the markings on the inside of your cone should look when it's ready.

just right, black lines and
blue lines matched

Below are examples of some mistakes to avoid:

too much overlap

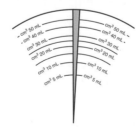

black lines matched at
bottom, but not at top

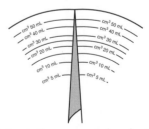

black lines matched at
top, but not at bottom

black lines not matched

some blue lines matched,
but not to the same measures

blue lines
not matched

The Weights and Diameters of Sports Balls ◀ MASTER 79

Ball	Diameter (cm)	Mass (g)
table-tennis	*3.8*	*2.5*

Use with Lesson 107.   **Unit 10**

Videotape Data: How Fast Do People Walk?

1	29	13.2	13
2	25	11.9	12
3	24	10.9	11
4	32	13.8	14
5	25	11.1	11
6	21	10.2	10
7	23	11.4	11.5
8	Do not use: jogging		
9	25	11.8	12
10	27	11.6	11.5
11	27	11.8	12

12	22	11.6	11.5
13	20	9.6	9.5
14	22	10.5	10.5
15	Do not use: walking dog		
16	18	9.1	9
17	23	11.6	11.5
18	21	10.1	10
19	Do not use: stilts		
20	22	10.1	10
21	25	11.4	11.5
22	23	12.1	12

1	29	13.2	13
2	25	11.9	12
3	24	10.9	11
4	32	13.8	14
5	25	11.1	11
6	21	10.2	10
7	23	11.4	11.5
8	Do not use: jogging		
9	25	11.8	12
10	27	11.6	11.5
11	27	11.4	11.5

12	22	11.6	11.5
13	20	9.6	9.5
14	22	10.5	10.5
15	Do not use: walking dog		
16	18	9.1	9
17	23	11.6	11.5
18	21	10.1	10
19	Do not use: stilts		
20	22	10.1	10
21	25	11.4	11.5
22	23	12.1	12

✔ Checking Progress

1. Complete each sentence with one of the following names of geometric solids:

     square pyramid   **cone**   **rectangular prism**   **cylinder**

   a. I have two bases and no vertices. I am a _____.

   b. I have exactly one base.
      All of my faces are triangular. I am a _____.

   c. I have six faces. All of them are rectangular. I am a _____.

   d. I have one flat face and one vertex. I am a _____.

2. The prism at the right is made of centimeter cubes.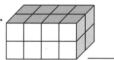

   a. What is the area of the base of the prism? _____

   b. What is the height of the prism?   _____

   c. What is the volume of the prism?   _____

   d. If you kept the base the same, but tripled the
      volume of this prism, what would be the height? _____

3.   **a.** Which of the boxes below has the greatest volume? _____

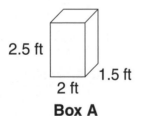

       2.5 ft   2 ft   2 ft
           1.5 ft   2 ft   1 ft
       2 ft   2 ft   3 ft
      Box A   **Box B**   **Box C**

   b. What is its volume? _____

4. The rectangular prism at the right has a
    volume of 120 in³.

    What is its height? _____

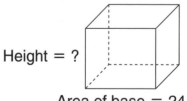

Height = ?

Area of base = 24 in²

✔ Checking Progress (continued)

Formulas

Area of circle $= \pi * r^2$

Volume of cylinder $=$ Area of base $*$ height

5. **a.** What is the area of the
base of the cylinder at the right? _____

    b. What is the volume of the cylinder?

    _____

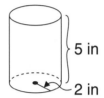

5 in

2 in

6. The pyramid at the right has the same
height as the prism in Problem 4 on Master 81.

What is the volume of the pyramid? _____

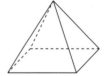

Area of base $= 24$ in^2

7. Circle the best estimate of the capacity of a soft-drink can.

    5 mL $\frac{1}{3}$ liter   2 liters

8. Joan wants to add medicine to her fish tank. The
instructions suggest adding one drop of medicine
for every 4 liters of water. The base of Joan's
fish tank measures 40 cm by 25 cm. The tank is
filled with water to a height of about 20 centimeters.

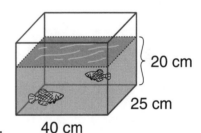

20 cm

25 cm

40 cm

    a. How many drops of medicine
should Joan add to her tank?   _____

Reminder

1 liter $= 1000$ cm^3

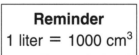

    b. Explain what you did to find the answer.

_____

_____

_____

_____

Unit 11

Fraction Multiplication, Percents, & Rates

Study Link: Parent Letter

Unit 11: Fraction Multiplication, Percents, and Rates

In Unit 11, your child will review and learn further how to multiply fractions and mixed numbers. *Everyday Mathematics* wants children to understand why they are doing certain algorithms, as well as to know how to do them. Therefore, students will have varied exposures to fraction and mixed-number multiplication.

Students will be introduced to fraction multiplication, using folded paper to represent fractions of a whole. Then the class will study fractions using "area models," which are diagrams that help students visualize dividing a "whole" into parts. This concept-building will lead to an algorithm for multiplying fractions:

$$\frac{a}{b} * \frac{c}{d} = \frac{a*c}{b*d}$$

Example: $\frac{2}{3} * \frac{3}{8} = \frac{2*3}{3*8} = \frac{6}{24}$ or $\frac{1}{4}$

For mixed-number multiplication the partial-products method is an easy way to do the computation. For example, $2\frac{1}{2} * 1\frac{2}{3}$ can be thought of as $(2 + \frac{1}{2}) * (1 + \frac{2}{3})$.

$$(\quad 2 \quad + \quad \frac{1}{2} \quad) * (\quad 1 \quad + \quad \frac{2}{3} \quad)$$

$$2 * 1 = 2$$
$$2 * \frac{2}{3} = \frac{4}{3}$$
$$\frac{1}{2} * 1 = \frac{1}{2}$$
$$\frac{1}{2} * \frac{2}{3} = \frac{2}{6}$$

partial products

$$2 + \frac{4}{3} + \frac{1}{2} + \frac{2}{6} = 4\frac{1}{6}$$

sum of partial products

The class will also review concepts introduced in earlier grades and expand on them. Students' experiences of area will be expanded to include mixed-number and fractional dimensions. Percent conversions will be reviewed. Estimating and figuring discounts will be introduced.

Opportunities to apply these concepts to real-world situations will be provided. Finding store discounts, working with recipes, examining sports players' scores, tracking pulse rates, and interpreting data about bicycle pedaling from a videotape will be among the applications.

You can help your child by asking questions about homework problems, by pointing out fractions and percents that you encounter in everyday life, and by playing the many versions of *Frac-Tac-Toe,* which was introduced in Unit 4, to sharpen conversion skills.

Study Link 116: "What's My Rule?"

1. Use the given rule to complete each table.

a.
Rule
$\triangle = \square * \frac{3}{5}$

in ($\square$)	out ($\triangle$)
$\frac{1}{2}$	_____
2	_____
$\frac{4}{5}$	_____
$\frac{3}{4}$	_____
3	_____

b.
Rule
$\triangle = \square * 4$

in ($\square$)	out ($\triangle$)
$\frac{2}{3}$	_____
$\frac{4}{5}$	_____
$\frac{8}{9}$	_____
$\frac{5}{4}$	_____
$\frac{7}{3}$	_____

2. What is the rule for each table?

a.
Rule

in ($\square$)	out ($\triangle$)
$\frac{2}{3}$	$\frac{2}{6}$
$\frac{3}{4}$	$\frac{3}{8}$
$\frac{7}{8}$	$\frac{7}{16}$
3	$1\frac{1}{2}$

b.
Rule

in ($\square$)	out ($\triangle$)
2	$\frac{1}{2}$
3	$\frac{3}{4}$
$\frac{5}{6}$	$\frac{5}{24}$
$\frac{2}{3}$	$\frac{1}{6}$

3. Make your own "What's My Rule?" table on the back of this page.

Study Link 117: Multiplying Fractions and Mixed Numbers

1. Multiply.

   a. $5\frac{3}{4} * \frac{2}{6} =$ _____

   b. $\frac{5}{8} * \frac{2}{5} =$ _____

   c. $4\frac{1}{4} * \frac{5}{6} =$ _____

   d. $2\frac{1}{3} * 3\frac{1}{8} =$ _____

   e. $3\frac{1}{12} * 1\frac{3}{5} =$ _____

   f. $2\frac{4}{5} * 3\frac{8}{2} =$ _____

2. Find the area of each figure below.

Area of a rectangle	Area of a triangle	Area of a parallelogram
$A = b * h$	$A = \frac{1}{2} * b * h$	$A = b * h$

a.

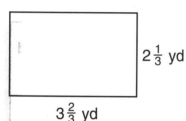

$2\frac{1}{3}$ yd

$3\frac{2}{3}$ yd

Area = _____ yd²

b.

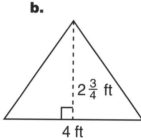

$2\frac{3}{4}$ ft

4 ft

Area = _____ ft²

c.

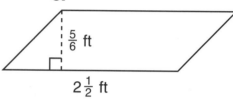

$\frac{5}{6}$ ft

$2\frac{1}{2}$ ft

Area = _____ ft²

3. The dimensions of a large doghouse are $2\frac{1}{2}$ times the dimensions of a small doghouse.

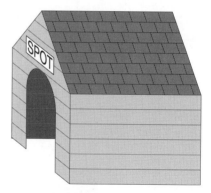

   a. If the width of the small doghouse is 2 feet, what is the width of the large doghouse?

   _____ feet

   b. If the length of the small doghouse is $2\frac{1}{4}$ feet, what is the length of the large doghouse?

   _____ feet

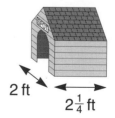

2 ft

$2\frac{1}{4}$ ft

Study Link 118: Fractions, Decimals, and Percents

1. Complete the table so that each number is shown as a fraction, decimal, and percent.

Fraction	Decimal	Percent
		45%
	0.3	
$\frac{2}{10}$		
	0.15	

2. Use your percent sense to estimate the discount for each item. Then calculate the discount for each item. (If necessary, round to the nearest cent.)

Item	List Price	Percent of Discount	Estimated Discount	Calculated Discount
Saguaro Cactus with Arms	$400.00	25%		
Life-sized Wax Figure of Yourself	$10,000.00	16%		
Manhole Cover	$78.35	10%		
Live Scorpion	$14.98	5%		
10,000 Honeybees	$29.00	30%		
Dinner for One on the Eiffel Tower	$88.00	6%		
Magician's Box for Sawing a Person in Half	$4,500.00	18%		
Fire Hydrant	$1,100.00	35%		

Source: *Everything Has Its Price.*

Study Link 119: Your Pulse; Unit Fractions

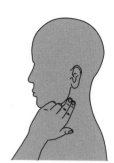

Practice taking your own pulse and the pulse of someone else at home. You can feel your pulse on your wrist below the thumb. You can also feel it in your neck: Run your index and middle fingers from the ear, past the curve of the jaw, and press them into the soft part of the neck just below the jaw.

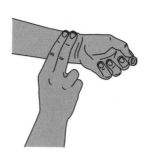

Were you able to find your pulse more easily at your wrist or neck? _____

Finding the worth of the unit fraction will help you to solve each problem below.

1. Neil's box of mixed fruit contains 15 oranges. These oranges are worth $\frac{3}{5}$ of the total pieces of fruit in his box. How many pieces of fruit does he have? _____ pieces

2. Grandma baked cookies. Of these cookies, 20 were oatmeal raisin. The oatmeal raisin cookies represent $\frac{5}{8}$ of all the cookies. How many cookies did Grandma bake? _____ cookies

3. Tiana jogged $\frac{6}{8}$ of the way to school in 12 minutes. If she continues at the same speed, how long will her entire jog to school take? _____ minutes

4. After 35 minutes, Hayden had completed $\frac{7}{10}$ of his math test. If he has a total of 55 minutes to complete the test, do you think he will finish on time? _____

5. Ian bought a video game that was on sale for $45. He paid 75% of the original price. How much would the game cost if it were not on sale? $ _____

6. An ad for a computer printer stated that you could buy the printer for only $280, or 80% of the original price. What was the original price of the printer? $ _____

How much would you save? $ _____

Study Link 120: An Apple for the Teacher

It is a long-standing tradition in the United States for students to give an apple to the teacher. In 1991, Tom Heymann researched what kind of apples elementary school teachers like to receive. He reported his findings in the book, *Unofficial U.S. Census.* He discovered that teachers preferred certain kinds of apples.

1. Calculate the following percents. Round to the nearest whole percent.

   a. Out of every 1500 teachers, about 1395 like apples.
       What percent of teachers like apples?   _____%

   b. Out of every 1395 teachers who like apples, about 300
       prefer Granny Smith. What percent of teachers prefer
       Granny Smith apples?   _____%

   c. Out of every 1395 teachers who like apples, about 360
       prefer Golden Delicious. What percent of teachers prefer
       Golden Delicious apples?   _____%

   d. Out of every 1395 teachers who like apples, about 150
       prefer McIntosh. What percent of teachers prefer
       McIntosh apples?   _____%

   e. Out of every 1395 teachers who like apples, about 585
       prefer Red Delicious. What percent of teachers prefer
       Red Delicious apples?   _____%

2. Multiply.

   a. $\frac{1}{2} * \frac{3}{4} =$ _____   **b.** $7 * \frac{5}{8} =$ _____

   c. $2\frac{1}{4} * \frac{3}{4} =$ _____   **d.** $1\frac{1}{4} * 3\frac{2}{5} =$ _____

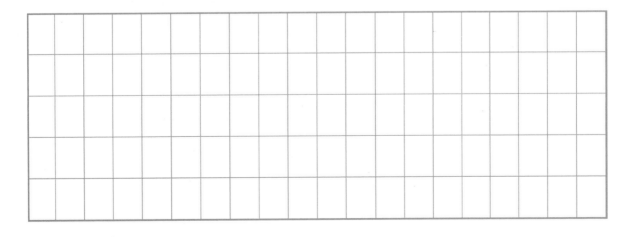

Study Link 121: Rate and Pan-Balance Problems

1. The average American eats about 250 eggs per year. At
   this rate, about how many eggs will the average American
   eat in five years?   _____

   In $\frac{1}{12}$ of a year?   _____

2. The average fifth grader can eat $\frac{3}{8}$ of a pizza for lunch.
   At this rate how many lunches will it take for an average
   fifth grader to eat the equivalent of 3 whole pizzas?   _____

3. In 1975, a man in Washington state ate 424 clams in
   8 minutes. At this rate, how many would he swallow in
   $\frac{1}{4}$ of this time?   _____

   How many could he swallow in $2\frac{1}{2}$ times as much time?   _____

4. Solve the following pan-balance problems:

   a.

   One circle weighs as much as   One square weighs as much as

   _____ triangles.   _____ triangles.

   b.

   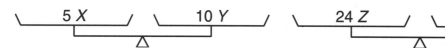 

   One X weighs as much as   One Y weighs as much as

   _____ Y's.   _____ Z's.

Study Link 122: Musical Ratios

Piano	21 million
Guitar	19 million
Organ	6 million
Flute	4 million
Clarinet	4 million
Drums	3 million
Trumpet	3 million
Violin	2 million
Harmonica	1.7 million
Saxophone	1 million
Electronic keyboard	0.6 million

At the left is a list of musical instruments played by people living in the United States and the approximate number of these people who play each instrument.

Source: *America by the Numbers.*

1. **a.** What is the ratio of flute players to harmonica players? _____

   b. What is the ratio of drum players to piano players? _____

   c. Record the ratio of violin and saxophone players to trumpet players. _____

2. Which two pairs of instrument players have a 1-to-1 ratio? _____

   _____

3. In a fifth-grade band, the ratio of saxophonists to clarinetists is 2:3. If there are 10 saxophonists, how many clarinetists are there? _____

Challenge

4. The school orchestra is performing tonight. There are 24 orchestra members. There are 6 violas. The ratio of violins to violas is 2:1. The ratio of cellos to basses is 2:1. There are no other instruments. How many chairs are needed in each section?

   violins _____   violas _____

   cellos _____   basses _____

Study Link 123: Traveling by Bicycle

1. In 1885, the bicycle was invented in England by James Starley. How many years ago was the bicycle invented? _____ years

2. A survey conducted by the National Sporting Goods Association in 1993 showed that bicycle riding ranked third as a physical activity in the United States with an estimated 53,972,000 people participating. Walking was ranked number one, with 10,028,000 more participants. What is the estimated number of people in the United States who chose walking as an activity? _____ people

3. Before World War II, the American bicycle weighed between 60 and 75 pounds. Today, some expensive racing bicycles weigh as little as 15 pounds. About how much is the difference in weight between what was available then and what is available now? _____ pounds

4. In heavy traffic a bicyclist can expect to travel at a speed of about 10 mph and in light traffic at about 15 mph.

   a. In heavy traffic, about how long would it take a bicyclist to complete a trip of 5 miles? _____

   b. In heavy traffic, about how long would it take a bicyclist to complete a trip of 12.5 miles? _____

   c. In light traffic, about how long would it take a bicyclist to complete a trip of $8\frac{3}{4}$ miles? _____

5. Regular cycling burns about 300 calories per hour and hill climbing or racing about 600 calories per hour.

   a. What is your favorite snack food? _____

   b. About how many calories are in one serving of this food? _____

   c. About how long would you need to bicycle to burn off one serving of this food if it were a regular cycling trip? _____

   And if you were hill climbing or racing? _____

Study Link 124: +, –, and * Fractions

1. In the Malagasay Indian tribes, it is against the law for a son to be taller than his father. If a son is taller, he must give his father money or an ox. Suppose a father is 5 feet $10\frac{1}{2}$ inches tall and the son is 5 feet $6\frac{3}{4}$ inches tall. How many more inches can the son grow before he is as tall as his father?

_____ in

2. In the state of Indiana, it is illegal to travel on a bus within 4 hours of eating garlic. If you had eaten a bowl of pasta with garlic bread $2\frac{1}{3}$ hours ago, how many more hours do you need to wait before you can legally travel on a bus?

_____ hr

3. In Idaho, it is against the law to give a person a box of candy that weighs more than 50 pounds. It is Valentine's Day and you give your mother a box of candy that weighs $48\frac{1}{4}$ pounds. How much more could the box weigh without breaking the law?

_____ lb

4. The body of an average jellyfish is about $\frac{9}{10}$ water. What fraction of the jellyfish is not water?

_____

5. The world record for a jump by a frog is 19 feet $3\frac{1}{8}$ inches. How much farther would a frog need to jump to set a new world record of 7 yards?

_____ in

6. The maximum length for a typical king cobra is about $5\frac{4}{5}$ meters. If 6 of these snakes were lined up end to end, how far would they stretch?

_____ m

7. An average trumpeter swan weighs about $16\frac{4}{5}$ kilograms. What is the approximate weight of 3 average trumpeter swans?

_____ kg

Sources: *Beyond Belief!! The Top 10 of Everything.*

Study Link 125: Parent Letter

Your child participated in a rich mathematics program during the past year. Our class explored a wide range of topics in order to encourage each child's curiosity about everyday life. Links between mathematics and the world were emphasized in our study of fractions and decimals, geometry, data collection and analysis, algorithms, patterns and sequences, and algebra. These topics will be studied in greater depth in sixth grade.

You can greatly affect your child's mathematical proficiency next year by practicing skills over the summer. Encourage your child's awareness of mathematics when shopping, planning a trip, cooking, participating in sports, ordering a meal, setting a schedule for the day, and so on.

Here are suggestions for activities you and your child can do together.

1. Review multiplication facts, especially those with products greater than 10, such as $7 * 8 = 56$. Include "extended facts," such as $70 * 8 = 560$ and $70 * 80 = 5600$.

2. Create opportunities for your child to work with rulers, yardsticks, metersticks, measuring tapes, and scales. Measure with both metric and U.S. customary units.

3. Play games introduced this year, such as *Factor Captor, Frac-Tac-Toe,* and *Multiplication Bull's-eye,* as well as old favorites such as *Multiplication Baseball* and *Calculator 10,000.*

4. Provide problems that involve multiplication and division, sometimes with numbers that are suitable for paper-and-pencil algorithms, and sometimes with complicated information appropriate for a calculator.

5. Practice using percents with sales tax, discounts, sports performance, and so on.

6. Continue the American Tour by reading about important people, events, inventions, explorations, and other topics in American history.

Best wishes for an enjoyable and rewarding summer!

Permission Slips

In math class, we plan to examine the effect of exercise on heart rate. Each student will find his or her heart rate after stepping up on and down from a stool or chair 5 times—and then 10, 15, 20, and 25 times.

Although the activity is not especially strenuous, we ask that you complete this form giving permission for your child's participation.

The data we collect will be used to teach graphing and other statistical skills.

I give permission for _____ to participate in the heart-rate activity described above.

Signature _____ Date _____

In math class, we plan to examine the effect of exercise on heart rate. Each student will find his or her heart rate after stepping up on and down from a stool or chair 5 times—and then 10, 15, 20, and 25 times.

Although the activity is not especially strenuous, we ask that you complete this form giving permission for your child's participation.

The data we collect will be used to teach graphing and other statistical skills.

I give permission for _____ to participate in the heart-rate activity described above.

Signature _____ Date _____

In math class, we plan to examine the effect of exercise on heart rate. Each student will find his or her heart rate after stepping up on and down from a stool or chair 5 times—and then 10, 15, 20, and 25 times.

Although the activity is not especially strenuous, we ask that you complete this form giving permission for your child's participation.

The data we collect will be used to teach graphing and other statistical skills.

I give permission for _____ to participate in the heart-rate activity described above.

Signature _____ Date _____

✔ Checking Progress, Part 1

1. The coach wants to divide 24 students evenly into teams for relay races. He wants the same number on each team, and no one left out. He knows that he can divide the students into 2 teams of 12 players each. What are two other ways he can form teams?

   a. _____ teams of _____ players   **b.** _____ teams of _____ players

2. A package of hot-dog buns contains 12 buns. Mrs. Hudson is expecting 35 people at her picnic. She wants to have enough hot dog buns for each person to have 2. How many packages of buns should she buy? _____

3. Jianhua buys a carton of milk for 59 cents, a hamburger for $1.25, and a salad for $1.50. He pays with a five-dollar bill.

   a. How much did he spend? _____

   b. How much change should he get? _____

4. Use your Geometry Template. Draw a polygon to fit each description below.

   a. A polygon with all sides the same length

   b. A polygon with acute and obtuse angles

5. **a.** Does the large hexagon on the Geometry Template tessellate? _____

   Support your answer with a drawing on the back of this page.

   b. What is the measure of each angle of this hexagon? _____

© 1999 Everyday Learning Corporation

✔ Checking Progress, Part 2

6. Below is a data set. Put two more numbers in it, so that

• the median of the new data set is 5

• the maximum is 15

• the range is 13

4,   5,   4,   11,   8,   _____,   _____

7. Solve the following problems. You can use the ruler on your Geometry Template to help you.

a. $\frac{1}{2} + \frac{1}{4} + \frac{1}{8} =$ _____

b. A board is $6\frac{1}{8}$ inches long. If you cut off $\frac{3}{4}$ of an inch, how much is left? _____

8. Jean combined $\frac{1}{3}$ cup of corn flour with $\frac{3}{4}$ cup of white flour.

a. Is the total amount of flour more or less than 1 cup? _____

Explain your answer. _____

_____

_____

b. If Jean wanted to triple the recipe (multiply the amount of each ingredient by 3), how many cups of each type of flour would she need?

_____ cup(s) corn flour   _____ cup(s) white flour

9. Match each fraction with its decimal or percent name.

$\frac{4}{8}$ 12%

$\frac{3}{25}$ 1.8

$\frac{9}{5}$ 50%

$\frac{4}{6}$ 0.95

$\frac{19}{20}$ $0.\overline{6}$

✔ Checking Progress, Part 3

10. Each square in the grid below has an area of 1 square centimeter.

    a. What is the area of triangle *END*? _____ cm²

    b. Draw a rectangle that has an area of 12 cm².

    c. What is the perimeter of this rectangle? _____ cm

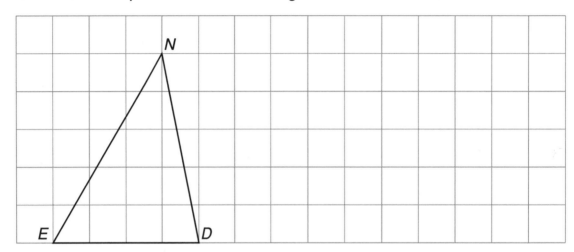

11. A cylindrical can has a base with an area of 21.5 square centimeters. It has a height of 10 centimeters. What is its volume?

    Volume of a Cylinder $V = B * h$

_____

12. a. Write the following number with digits:

    one billion, twelve million, forty-one thousand, twelve

_____

    b. If you subtract 10 thousand from the number in Part **a,** what is the result?

_____

13. a. Use the rule below to complete the table at the right.

Rule
$D = t + 12$

t	D
15	
8	
	12
−12	

    b. *D* is exactly twice the value of *t* when

    $D =$ _____ and $t =$ _____

✔ Checking Progress, Part 4

14. Mr. Taylor's science class asked 50 students each to name their favorite pet. The results are in the table at the right.

Animal	Number	Percent
Cat	21	
Dog	13	
Hamster or Gerbil	4	
Bird	8	
Other	4	
Total	50	

a. Complete the percent column in the table.

b. How many students in all named either
cat or **dog** as their favorite pet? _____ students

c. Did **more than half** or **less than half** of the
students name cat as their favorite pet? _____

d. What pet was named by about $\frac{1}{4}$ of the students? _____

e. What percent named **snake** as their favorite pet? (Circle the best answer.)

     4%   not more than 8%   at least 4 of the students

15. Draw a circle graph of the information in Problem 14. Label each section. Use your Geometry Template.

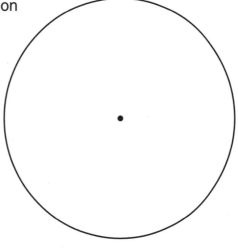

Favorite Pets

Review Masters

Number Theory

1. Draw as many different rectangular arrays as you can using 16 objects.

2. **a.** Name all of the factors of 28. _____

   b. Name all of the factors of 18. _____

   c. Name all of the factors of 17. _____

3. **a.** Name two numbers that are divisible by 2 and 9. _____

   b. Name two numbers that are divisible by 3 and 5. _____

   c. Name a number that is divisible by 3, 5, and 9. _____

4. **a.** Circle the square numbers in this list: 7   22   9   36   12   225

   b. How do you know that they are square numbers?

   _____

   _____

5. Explain why you agree or disagree with the following statement: It is not possible for a number to be a square number and a composite number.

   _____

   _____

Place Value and Computation

1. Write the number described below.

- Double 14. Subtract 10. Divide by 9. The answer is the digit in the **tenths** place.

- If you multiply the digit in the **hundreds** place by 60, the answer is 540.

- The digit in the **ones** place is the same as the number of sides of a pentagon.

- Multiply 9 times 4. Subtract the value of 6^2. The answer is the digit in the **tens** place.

- If you multiply the digit in the **hundredths** place by 1, the answer is 1.

- The digit in the **thousands** place is $\frac{2}{3}$ of the digit in the hundreds place.

What is the number? ____ ____ ____ ____ . ____ ____

2. Compute.

a. $347 + 496 =$ _____   **b.** $931 - 23 =$ _____

c. $34.7 + 18.4 =$ _____   **d.** $101.3 - 94.6 =$ _____

e. $23 * 67 =$ _____   **f.** $342 * 7 =$ _____

Fractions, Decimals, and Percents

1. Complete each row in the table at the right with equivalent numbers.

Fraction	Decimal	Percent
$\frac{9}{100}$		
	0.01	
		80%
$\frac{3}{4}$		
	0.95	
		50%
$\frac{1}{5}$		
	0.30	
		10%

2. Write four equivalent fractions or mixed numbers for each of the following.

a. $\frac{2}{3}$, _____, _____, _____, _____

b. $\frac{5}{8}$, _____, _____, _____, _____

c. $3\frac{2}{5}$, _____, _____, _____, _____

d. $\frac{1}{10}$, _____, _____, _____, _____

e. $1\frac{7}{10}$, _____, _____, _____, _____

3. Use your Percent Circle to find what percent each piece of these circle graphs represents. Write each answer in or near the piece.

a.   **b.**   **c.**

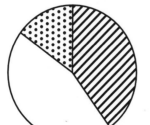 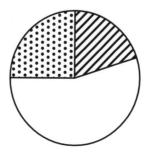 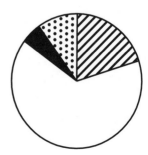

Fraction and Percent Multiplication

1. Complete the following.

    a. 30% of 50 is _____.   **b.** 25% of 36 is _____.   **c.** 5% of 150 is _____.

    d. 75% of 12 is _____.   **e.** 80% of 60 is _____.   **f.** 50% of 130 is _____.

2. Find the whole.

    a. 50% of _____ is 12.   **b.** $\frac{3}{4}$ of _____ is 21.   **c.** 90% of _____ is 180.

    d. $\frac{5}{6}$ of _____ is 25.   **e.** 20% of _____ is 19.   **f.** $\frac{3}{8}$ of _____ is 24.

3. Multiply.

    a. $\frac{1}{2} * \frac{3}{4} =$ _____   **b.** $2\frac{3}{4} * \frac{3}{5} =$ _____   **c.** $1\frac{1}{2} * 2\frac{1}{4} =$ _____

    d. $\frac{3}{4} * 5 =$ _____   **e.** $7 * \frac{4}{5} =$ _____   **f.** $\frac{5}{6} * \frac{1}{5} =$ _____

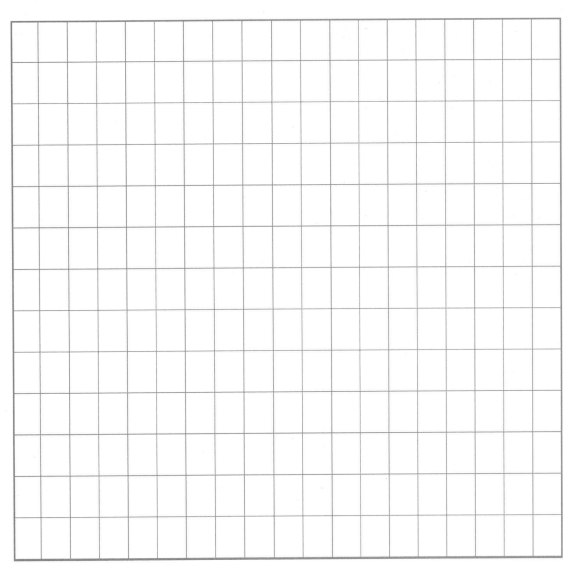

Year-End Review

Division, Ratios, and Exponential Notation

1. Use your favorite algorithm to divide.

   a. 160/8 =   **b.** 385/5 =   **c.** 272/4 =   **d.** 138/12 =

      _____   _____   _____   _____

   e. $7\overline{)422}$ **f.** $20\overline{)270}$ **g.** $15\overline{)365}$ **h.** $25\overline{)574}$

2. Write a number sentence and solution for the following problems. Decide what to do with any remainders. Circle your answer.

   a. Marcia has $87 to spend on CDs. Each CD costs $12. How many CDs can she buy?

     Number Sentence _____ Solution _____

     Ignore remainder.   Round answer up.   Report remainder as a fraction.

   b. Abdul wants to play 8 different games on his computer. He has 3 hours of free time in which to play. If he wants to play each game for the same length of time, how many minutes should he play each game?

     Number Sentence _____ Solution _____

     Ignore remainder.   Round answer up.   Report remainder as a fraction.

   c. Esmeralda has a collection of 296 decorated eggs. She painted 87 of them herself. She plans to buy special containers to keep her eggs safe. Each container holds 12 eggs. How many containers does she need?

     Number Sentence _____ Solution _____

     Ignore remainder.   Round answer up.   Report remainder as a fraction.

3. The average American drinks about 6000 glasses of juice in a lifetime.
    About 2600 of those are orange juice. Express the ratio of orange juice
    to all juices with

    a fraction. _____   a percent. _____   a colon. _____

    words. _____

4. Complete the table below. The first row is done for you.

Exponential Notation	Base	Exponent	Repeated Factors	Product
8^4	8	4	8 * 8 * 8 * 8	4096
	4	5		
			9 * 9 * 9	
	7	4		

5. Make each sentence true by inserting parentheses.

    a. 15 + 4 − 3 * 2 = 13   **b.** 15 + 4 − 3 * 2 = 32

    c. 15 + 4 − 3 * 2 = 17   **d.** 9 = 9 + 9 / 3 − 1

    e. 11 = 9 + 9 / 3 − 1   **f.** 24 / 6 + 2 = 6

    g. 24 / 6 + 2 = 3   **h.** 3 * 4 + 4 / 2 = 18

6. Match each number story with the number sentence that represents the
    information.

    Number of cookies left on the trays

    Story 1
    Larry baked 7 trays of chocolate
    chip cookies. Each tray had 8 cookies.   7 * (8 − 6) = 14
    Larry ate 6 of the cookies.

    Story 2
    Larry baked 7 trays of chocolate chip
    cookies. Each tray had 8 cookies. He   (7 * 8) − 6 = 50
    took 6 cookies off each tray and gave
    them to his friends at school.

Year-End Review

Fractions and Ratios

1. a. Use your ruler to draw a line segment $2\frac{5}{8}$ inches long.

    b. If you erased $\frac{3}{4}$ inch from one end of your line segment,
        how long would the new line segment be?   _____ in

    c. If you drew a line segment that was $\frac{3}{4}$ of an inch longer
        than your original line segment, how long would the
        new line segment be?   _____ in

2. Mark each of the points on the ruler below. Write the letter above your mark.
Point *A* has been done for you.

    A: $3\frac{5}{8}$ in   *B:* $2\frac{3}{16}$ in   *C:* $\frac{7}{8}$ in

    D: $4\frac{2}{16}$ in   *E:* $1\frac{5}{16}$ in   *F:* $3\frac{15}{16}$ in

3. Complete these ruler puzzles.

    Example: $\frac{1}{4}$ in $= \frac{x}{8}$ in $= \frac{y}{16}$ in $x =$ ___2___ $y =$ ___4___

    a. $1\frac{2}{8}$ in $= 1\frac{x}{16}$ in $= 1\frac{y}{4}$ in $x =$ _____ $y =$ _____

    b. $3\frac{6}{8}$ in $= 3\frac{x}{4}$ in $= 3\frac{y}{16}$ in $x =$ _____ $y =$ _____

    c. $\frac{4}{8}$ in $= \frac{x}{16}$ in $= \frac{1}{y}$ in $x =$ _____ $y =$ _____

4. How many minutes does each fraction represent? The first one has been done
for you.

    a. $\frac{1}{6}$ hr $=$ ___*10 min*___   **b.** $\frac{8}{12}$ hr $=$ _____

    c. $\frac{2}{3}$ hr $=$ _____   **d.** $\frac{5}{12}$ hr $=$ _____

    e. $\frac{5}{4}$ hr $=$ _____   **f.** $\frac{5}{6}$ hr $=$ _____

Fractions and Ratios (continued)

5. Add or subtract.

a. $\frac{3}{8} + \frac{7}{8} =$ _____

b. $\frac{1}{6} + \frac{7}{12} =$ _____

c. $1\frac{1}{3} - \frac{5}{6} =$ _____

d. $\begin{array}{r} \frac{11}{12} \\ + \frac{3}{4} \\ \hline \end{array}$

e. $\begin{array}{r} 2\frac{5}{8} \\ - 1\frac{1}{4} \\ \hline \end{array}$

f. $\begin{array}{r} 3\frac{5}{12} \\ - 1\frac{2}{3} \\ \hline \end{array}$

6. Find a common denominator for each of the following. Then give the answer.

	Common Denominator	**Answer**
a. $\frac{1}{12} + \frac{3}{4} =$	_____	_____
b. $\frac{5}{6} + \frac{1}{9} =$	_____	_____
c. $\frac{2}{3} - \frac{3}{5} =$	_____	_____

7. Use your tiles from Lesson 99 to solve the following problems:

a. Place 12 white tiles on your desk.
Now add shaded tiles so that 1 out of 4 is shaded.

How many tiles are there in all? _____

b. Place 15 white tiles on your desk.
Now add shaded tiles so that 3 out of 5 are white.

How many tiles are there in all? _____

c. Place 24 tiles on your desk so that 15 are shaded.

_____ out of 8 tiles are shaded.

Collecting and Working with Data

1. Rafael surveyed his classmates to find out how many hours per week they spend doing homework. The graph below represents his data.

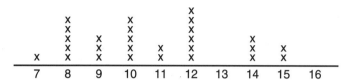

```
                        x
      x           x     x
      x           x     x
      x     x     x           x
      x     x     x     x     x     x     x
x     x     x     x     x     x     x     x
7     8     9    10    11    12    13    14    15    16
```

Rafael concluded that the average student in his class spends about 12 hours per week on homework. Do you agree or disagree with his conclusion? _____

Why? _____

_____

_____

2. On the first day of gym class, students did as many sit-ups as they could. During the year, they started each class with sit-ups. At the end of the year, they did as many sit-ups as they could.

Which stem-and-leaf plot below do you think represents the number of sit-ups students could do at the beginning of the year? _____

Why? _____

_____

Which stem-and-leaf plot below do you think represents the number of sit-ups students could do at the end of the year? _____

Why? _____

_____

Plot a		**Plot b**		**Plot c**		**Plot d**	
tens	ones	tens	ones	hundreds	tens	tens	ones
0	1 1 4 4 5 6 7 9	0		0		0	5
1	1 1 3 4 4 4	1		1		1	5 7 9 9
2	1 1	2		2	0 4 3 9	2	0 3 9 9
3		3	0 0 0 1 1 5 6	3	0 1 1 4 5 8	3	1 1 3 3 7 8
4		4	0 5 7 7 9	4	2 7 8 8	4	2 7 9
5		5	4 7 8	5	0 4 4	5	3 3 4 6
6	7 7	6	2	6	3 5 5 6 8	6	0 5 5
7		7	1	7	5 6	7	4
8		8	4 5 9	8	8	8	
9	2 3 3 3 4 5	9	0 2 2	9		9	
10		10	3 4	10		10	

Collecting and Working with Data (continued)

3. Roosevelt Middle School surveyed students to find out what they preferred for lunch in the cafeteria. The results were as follows:

Percent of Students	Preferred Lunch
10%	Grilled cheese sandwich
35%	Hamburger or cheeseburger
5%	Spaghetti
7%	Fried chicken
43%	Hot dog

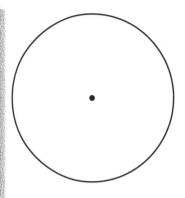

Use your Percent Circle to draw a circle graph of these data.

4. A fifth grade class collected the following data. The results are shown on number-line plots below. Write a letter next to each plot to match it with one of the descriptions.

(a) Number of pets at home

(b) Ages of brothers and sisters living at home

(c) Approximate number of books read during the past year
(rounded to the nearest 5 books)

(d) Average number of hours spent sleeping in a week
(rounded to the nearest 5 hours)

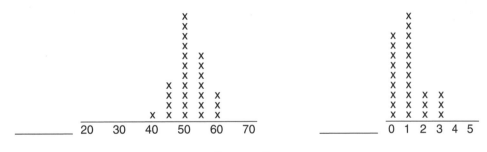

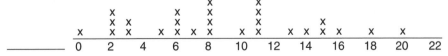

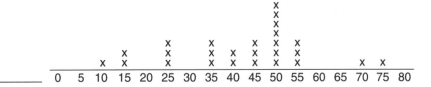

Geometry

Review 11

Think about each geometry word below.

If you can define it with words or by drawing a picture, circle it.

If you have some idea of what the word means, but aren't sure, underline it.

If you are not sure what the word means, don't mark it.

Parallel	Polygon	Rhombus	Obtuse angle
Right angle	Acute angle	Trapezoid	Cylinder
Parallelogram	Adjacent angles	Radius	Diameter
Equilateral triangle	Congruent	Protractor	Vertical angles
Tessellation	Perpendicular	Cone	Perimeter
Circumference	Square foot	Trapezoid	Vertex

1. Each riddle below describes a figure on your Geometry Template. On the right side of this page, use the Geometry Template to draw the figure. There may be more than one right answer.

    a. I am a polygon.
        I have an even number of sides.
        I have no right angles.
        I can tessellate.

    b. I am not a polygon.
        I am not a circle.
        I am a closed figure.

    c. I am a quadrilateral.
        Two of my angles are obtuse.
        Two of my angles are acute.
        My opposite angles are not equal.

    d. I am a polygon.
        I have a prime number of sides.
        All of my angles are obtuse.

2. Make up your own geometry riddle. Draw the shape that is the answer.

_____

_____

_____

3. Draw two copies of triangle T3 on the Geometry Template so that they form a parallelogram.

4. Look at triangle T4 on the Geometry Template. Then circle all of the statements below that are true about this shape.

All its sides are the same length.   It is an isosceles triangle.

All its angles are acute.   Two angles have the same measure.

It is a regular polygon.   It has 2 obtuse angles.

Coordinates and Distance

1.   **a.** Plot the following 3 points:

(1,2); (1, −3); (4,2)

Plot a fourth point so that the four
points are the vertices of a rectangle.

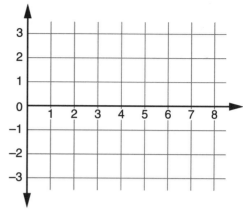

    b. What are the coordinates
       of the fourth vertex?   _____

2.   **a.** Estimate the distance along the path from
       the campground to the beach, as shown
       by the map below.

_____ km

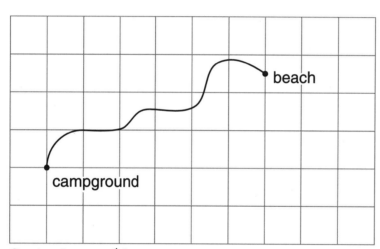

Scale: 1 cm to $\frac{1}{2}$ km

    b. Explain how you estimated the distance.

_____

_____

_____

_____

Area, Perimeter, and Circumference

> **Area of a rectangle** = length * width
> or
> $A = l * w$
> or
> $A = b * h$
> **Area of a circle** = pi * radius * radius
> or
> $A = \pi * r^2$
> **Circumference of a circle** = pi * diameter
> or
> $C = \pi * d$

1. Wanda is helping her mother to make a vegetable garden in the shape of a rectangle 4 feet by 8 feet.

8 ft
4 ft

    a. Wanda wants to put a fence around the vegetable garden. How many feet of fence does she need?   _____ ft

    b. What is the area of this garden? (Circle one.)

        32 ft   144 sq ft   32 sq ft   24 ft

    c. Wanda measured the side that is 4 feet long. How many inches is that?   _____ in

2. Wanda suggested making a flower garden in the shape of a square 6 feet by 6 feet.

6 ft
6 ft

    a. What will the area and perimeter of this garden be?

        Area   _____ ft^2

        Perimeter   _____ ft

    b. Wanda wants to plant roses at least 3 feet apart. What is the largest number of rose plants she can fit into the square flower garden?   _____

3. Wanda's friend Tim built a garden in the shape of circle.
The garden has a radius of 5 feet.

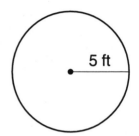

a. What is the area of the circle?

(Round the answer to the nearest tenth.) _____ ft²

b. Tim plans to put a fence around the garden.

How long will the fence be?
(Round the answer to the nearest tenth.) _____ ft

c. Tim thinks he might plant raspberry bushes in his
garden. If each bush is to have 5 square feet,
how many raspberry bushes should he buy? _____ bushes

Challenge

4. Divide the square at the bottom of this page into 3 triangles that have the
following properties:

- Two triangles have the same area.
- The third triangle has twice the area of either of the others.

Explain how you divided the square. _____

_____

_____

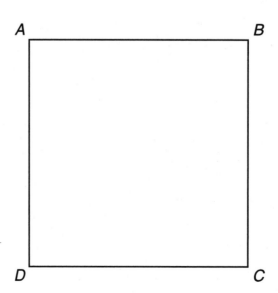

Volume and 3-Dimensional Shapes, Part 1

1. Circle all of the shapes below that are cylinders.

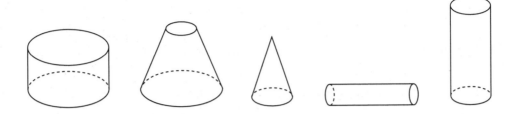

2. Circle all of the statements below that are true for cylinders:

(a) All surfaces are formed by circles.

(b) Faces are formed by congruent circles.

(c) There are 3 surfaces.

(d) There are 2 vertices.

3. Which of the following is a unit you might use in measuring the volume of a cone? Circle one.

inch   cubic centimeter   pound   square inch

4. Which of the following is a unit you might use in measuring the area of the base of a cylinder? Circle one.

square foot   liter   cubic inch   centimeter

Volume and 3-Dimensional Shapes, Part 2 Review 17

1. The shape at the bottom of this page can be cut out and folded into a rectangular prism. (If you wish, you may cut it out.) Each small square has an area of 1 cm^2.

    a. What is the area of the base of this rectangular prism? _____ cm^2

    b. If you fold up the sides, what will be the height of this prism? _____ cm

    c. What is the volume of this prism? _____ cm^3

    d. Give the dimensions of another prism that has the same volume.

    length _____ cm   width _____ cm   height _____cm

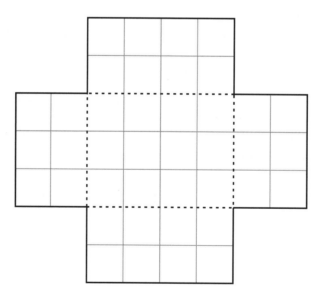

Volume and 3-Dimensional Shapes, Part 2 (continued)

2. Use the area and volume formulas below to answer the questions. Round answers to the nearest tenth.

> **Area of a circle** $= \pi * \text{radius} * \text{radius}$
> or
> $A = \pi * r^2$
> **Volume of a cylinder** $= \text{area of base} * \text{height}$
> or
> $V = B * h$

a. What is the area of the base of the cylinder?   _____ in^2

b. What is the volume of the cylinder?   _____ in^3

                                                            8 in

c. What is the area of the top face of the cylinder?   _____ in^2 4.5 in

3. Take a regular sheet of paper (8.5 inches by 11 inches). Roll it and tape the shorter edges together to form a cylinder.

a. What is the circumference of the base of this cylinder?   _____ in

b. What is the height of this cylinder?   _____ in

c. Find the following. Round to the nearest tenth.

diameter of the base   _____ in

radius of the base   _____ in

area of the base   _____ in^2

volume of the cylinder   _____ in^3

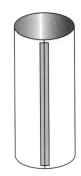

Year-End Review

Algebra Concepts and Skills

1. Add or subtract. You may use ⊞ and ⊟ counters.

     a. 35 + (−10) = _____   **b.** −40 + (−8) = _____   **c.** −18 + 12 = _____

     d. 19 − (−19) = _____   **e.** 45 + (−22) = _____   **f.** −32 − 14 = _____

2. Solve these pan-balance problems. In each figure, the pans are in perfect balance.

     a.

     One cube weighs as much as _____ marbles.

     b.

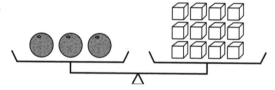

     One orange weighs as much as _____ cubes.

     c.

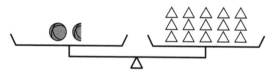

     One ball weighs as much as _____ triangles.

     d.

     One coin weighs as much as   One block weighs as much as

     _____ marbles.   _____ marbles.

Year-End Review

Algebra Concepts and Skills (continued)

3. Complete each statement with an algebraic expression, using the given variable. The first one is done for you.

   a. If Michael has $3.25 more than David, then

      Michael has   __*A* + *3.25*__   dollars.

David has *A* dollars.   Michael

   b. If Lisa is 7 inches taller than Jenell, then

      Lisa is _____ inches tall.

Jenell is *Q* inches tall.   Lisa

   c. From his home, Daniel rode his bike 8 kilometers past the school. He rode

      _____ kilometers in all.

home   school

D kilometers from home to school.

   d. Regina read $\frac{3}{4}$ of her book. She read

      _____ pages.

The book has *P* pages.

For each "What's My Rule?" table state the rule in words and as a number sentence.

4. Rule: _____

   _____

x	y
4	9
7	12
10	15
21	26
38	43

5. Rule: _____

   _____

s	t
4	2
9	4.5
12	6
20	10
35	17.5

Number sentence

_____

Number sentence

_____

Algebra Concepts and Skills (continued)

6. Complete the table. Then graph the data and connect the points.
When Robert watches television, he burns about 80 calories an hour.

Rule: Total calories burned = 80 * number of hours

Plot a point to show the number of calories burned in 5 hours.

About how many calories is that? _____

7. Each of the following graphs represents one of the events described below.
Match each event with its graph. (The horizontal axis represents time.)

Time (t) (hours)	Calories ($80 * t$)
1	80
2	
	320
	520
$8\frac{1}{2}$	

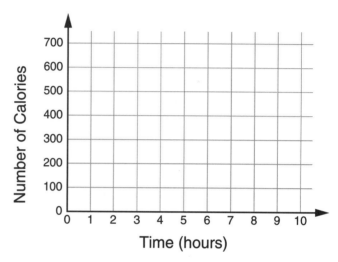

_____ Which graph shows the height of a flowering plant from the time it is
planted as a seed until it withers and dies?

_____ When air is heated, it expands. When air cools, it contracts. Which graph
shows the size of the balloon Jimmy is holding as he walks home from a
birthday party on a cold day?

_____ Frank is running a 26-mile marathon. Which graph shows his speed
during the race?

_____ Samantha's dog, Red, is fetching sticks in the backyard. Which graph
might show the distance between Samantha and her dog while they play?

Teaching Aids

Computation Grid

Teaching
Aid
1

Name That Number

Materials ❑ Make up a deck of number cards from an ordinary deck of playing cards, as follows:

- For the numbers 2 through 10, use the 2 through 10 cards.
- For the number 1, use aces.
- Write the number 0 on the queen face cards.
- Write the numbers 11 through 18 on the remaining face cards (kings, jacks).

Number of players 2 or 3

Directions Shuffle the deck of cards and deal 5 cards to each player. Turn over the top card. This is the **target number** for the round.

Players try to name the target number by adding, subtracting, multiplying, or dividing the numbers on as many of their cards as possible. A card can only be used once. They write their solutions on a sheet of paper or slate. Then they set aside the cards they used to name the target number and replace them with new cards from the top of the deck. They put the target number on the bottom of the deck and turn over the top card. This is the new target number.

Play continues until there are not enough cards left in the deck to replace both players' cards. The player who set aside more cards wins the game.

Sample turn:

Player's numbers: 7 5 8 2 10
Target number: 16

Some possible solutions:

7 × 2 = 14 → 14 + **10** = 24
→ 24 − **8** = 16

(four cards used)

8 ÷ 2 = 4 → 4 + **10** = 14
→ 14 + **7** = 21
→ 21 − **5** = 16

(all five cards used)

Name   Date   Time

Assessment Check-off Sheet

Teaching
Aid
3

Unit _____
Names							Comments
1.						
2.						
3.						
4.						
5.						
6.						
7.						
8.						
9.						
10.						
11.						
12.						
13.						
14.						
15.						
16.						
17.						
18.						
19.						
20.						
21.						
22.						
23.						
24.						
25.						
26.						
27.						
28.						
29.						
30.						

Cumulative Review Check-off Sheet

Names (Date)	Place Value and Numeration	Fractions and Decimals	Estimation and Measurement	Geometry	Operations (+ −) (× ÷)	Data and Graphing

Cumulative Review Check-off Sheet

Graph Paper ($\frac{1}{8}$-in Squares by 5s)

Teaching
Aid
5

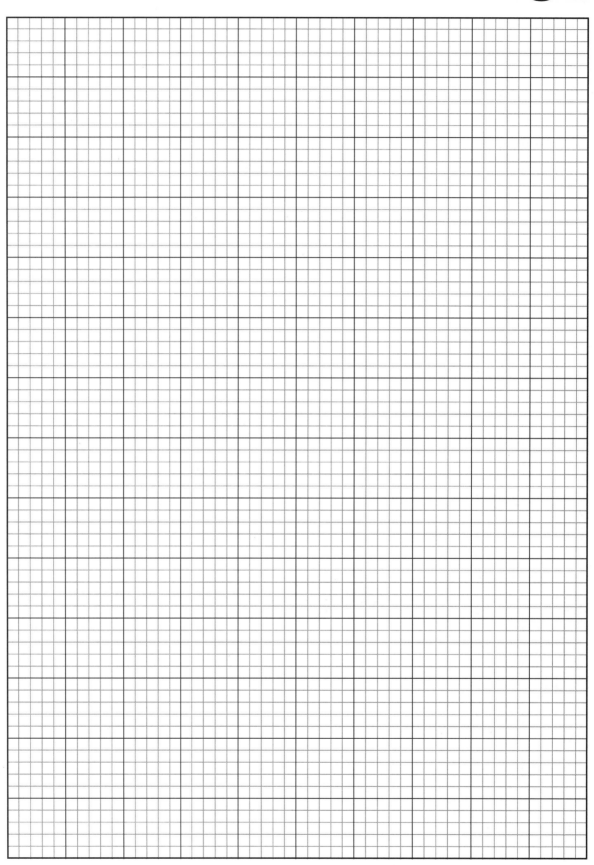

Graph Paper ($\frac{1}{8}$-in Squares by 4s)

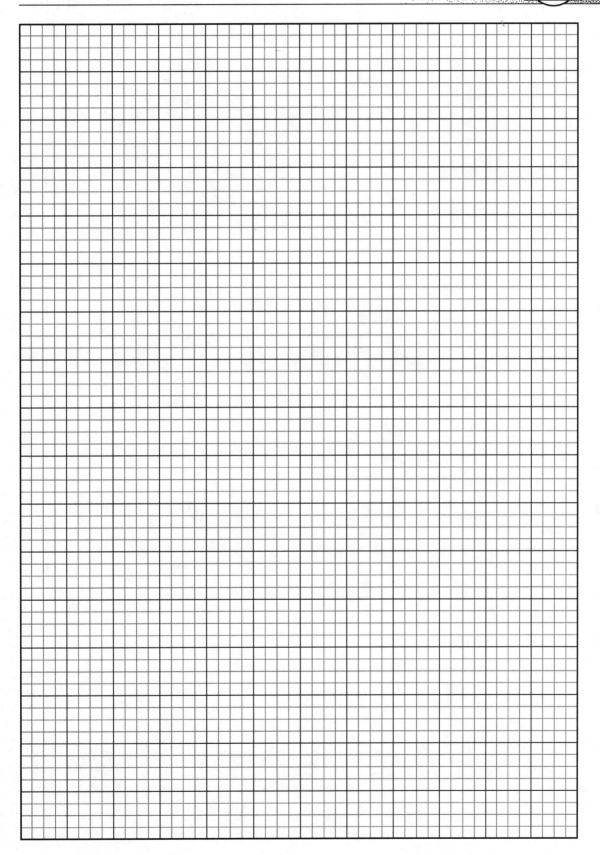

Grid Paper (1 in)

Grid Paper ($\frac{1}{4}$ in)

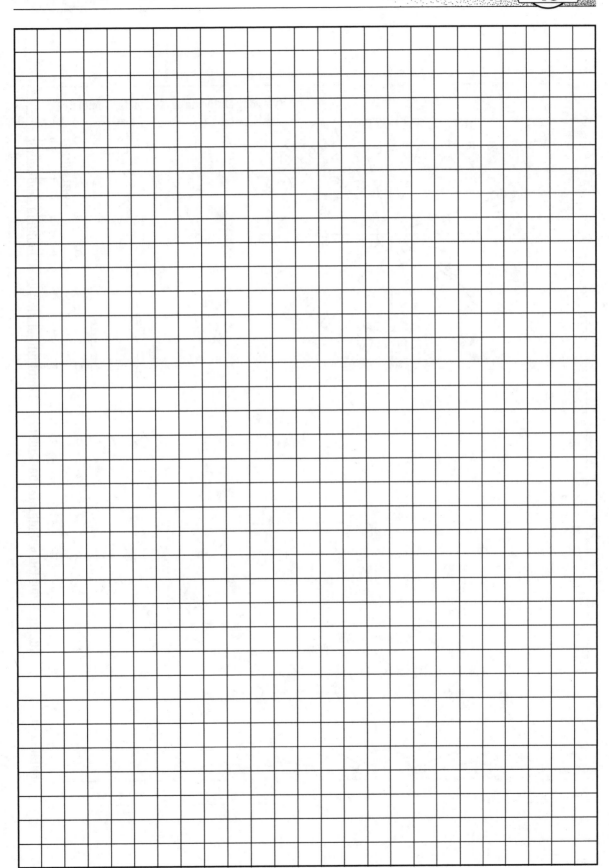

Geometry Template

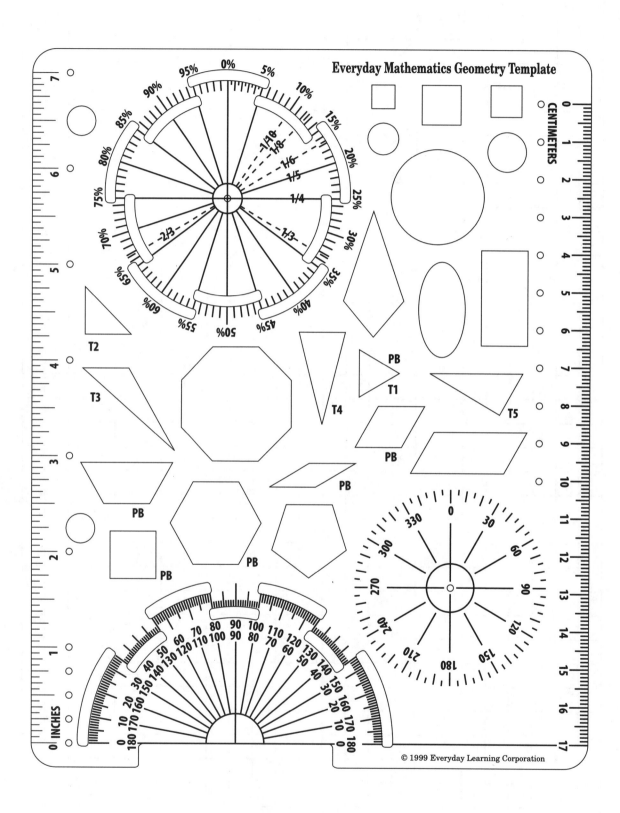

Everyday Mathematics Geometry Template

Notes for Lesson _____

Item No. 39507

ISBN 1-57039-507

EVERYDAY LEARNING™

Chicago, Illinois